Dedicated with love to my wife, Debbie

and my son, Joseph

ACKNOWLEDGEMENTS

I thank Dr. W. Keith Berg for his guidance, astute
judgement and his infectious positive approach to life.
His active support of our past and present collaborative
efforts has meant a great deal to me. I look forward to a
long and fruitful future association. As well, I thank you
for so willingly being there whenever I needed you and for
patiently allowing me to interrupt your stories of the joys
of fatherhood in order to tell you mine.

I would also like to express my appreciation to my
doctoral committee, Drs. Merle E. Meyer, Peter Lang, Phil
Posner and Neil Rowland, for their assistance throughout my
graduate training. Also, I thank Drs. Don Stehouwer and Paul
Davenport for their helpful comments on this project.

In addition, I thank all those infants who fell asleep
for me and most notably I thank all those little kids who
held their breath for me and even those that didn't. Also,
I am grateful to the parents of the little kids for
generously contributing their time to this effort.

Special thanks are extended to my assistants, Alonso,
Judy, Kristen, Karen, Julio and Yolanda, for their help in
data collection at various times throughout the past two

years. I thank my lab mates Terry Blumenthal, Margaret Davies and Allen Klempert for their enjoyable association and patient tolerance.

I thank my parents and the rest of my family for their tenacious support and everlasting expression of faith and encouragement. I stand tall because of them. Finally, to my wife and true friend Debbie, thank you for being there when I wasn't and also when I was, and more importantly thank you for my son, Joseph.

TABLE OF CONTENTS

LIST OF TABLES

LIST OF FIGURES

Abstract of Dissertation Presented to the Graduate School
of the University of Florida in Partial Fulfillment of the
Requirements for the Degree of Doctor of Philosophy

APNEA AND BRADYCARDIA ELICITED BY FACIAL AIRSTREAM
STIMULATION IN HEALTHY INFANTS IN THE FIRST YEAR OF LIFE:
IMPLICATIONS FOR DETECTION OF INFANTS AT RISK
FOR SUDDEN INFANT DEATH SYNDROME

By

BARRY ELLIOT HURWITZ

August, 1984

Chairman: W. Keith Berg
Major Department: Psychology

Cardiorespiratory responses to airstream stimulation
(10-seconds, 1.06 psi) were observed in 52 newborn (NB),
2-4 and 8-12 month-old healthy infants. Two areas of
stimulation were compared: the facial region, which
included the forehead, eyelids and nose, and the abdominal
region rostral to the umbilicus, which served as a control
stimulation site. The infants were tested while asleep,
during which EKG, heart rate and respiration were recorded.

The results revealed that in both NB and 2-4 month
infants, facial cooling with an airpuff elicited apnea with
greater frequency and duration than did the control
airpuff. Apnea occurred on about 27.2% of facial trials
compared to 7.8% of control trials. The duration of apnea

was twice as long in the 2-4 month infants as in the NBs. By 8-12 months the facial airpuff still elicited apnea more reliably than did the abdominal airpuff but with reduced frequency of 8.9% and 1.9% respectively. The duration of apnea, however, was maintained at the longer duration seen with the 2-4 month infants. Bradycardia on trials when apnea was elicited differed in magnitude between age groups such that the 2-4 and 8-12 month infants decelerated to about -15 bpm; whereas no bradycardic response to apnea was displayed by the NBs.

It has been demonstrated that in healthy sleeping NB and 2-4 month infants an airstream directed to the face can elicit apnea. However, by 8-12 months facial cooling does not have as great an effect on inhibition of respiration. Although apnea can be elicited in the NBs by facial airpuff, this apnea was brief and resulted in no change in cardiac response. Therefore, at 2-4 months, which is the age of greatest vulnerability for Sudden Infant Death Syndrome (SIDS), the airpuff was likely to produce more frequent, prolonged apnea with concomitant bradycardia. It has been suggested that SIDS infants produce prolonged apnea because they have a higher threshold for hypoxia. Therefore, by eliciting apnea with facial cooling, it may be possible to identify a predisposition to SIDS by analysis of the magnitude of cardiorespiratory change in infants with a history of prolonged apnea.

CHAPTER 1
INTRODUCTION

"and this woman's child died in the night,
because she overlaid it"

This quote, which is from an account in the Book of

Kings 3:16-28 circa tenth century B.C., in which the word

"overlaid" appeared to imply suffocation of an infant

during the night, has been cited as perhaps the first

recorded instance of Sudden Infant Death Syndrome (SIDS)

(Peterson, 1980). Despite it's probable antiquity, SIDS

was largely ignored by the scientific community until, as

infant mortality rates declined, it became apparent that

these deaths comprised a substantial proportion of all

infant deaths within the first year of life. Currently the

incidence of SIDS throughout the world varies from 0.6 to

3.0 deaths per 1000 live births, accounting for about

7-9,000 deaths each year in the United States alone

(Peterson, 1980; Valdes-Dapena, 1980). About one-third of

all deaths in infants between the ages of one week and one

year are diagnosed SIDS and it is the most frequent cause

of death in this age group (Moore, 1981).

Prior to 1963, deaths that occurred suddenly,

unexpectedly, and inexplicably with no recognizable lethal

pathology at autopsy were generally certified to one or

another cause-of-death category in keeping with the attending coroner's personal inclination (Peterson, 1980). This practice circumvented the embarassment of a factual "don't know" and at the same time complied with legal expectations. Following the 1963 conference on causes of SIDS, awareness and acceptance of sudden unexpected death as a legitimate diagnostic entity increased. Finally the designation, Sudden Infant Death Syndrome, emerged from the Second International SIDS Conference in 1969, wherein an occurrence of SIDS was defined as the sudden death of any infant which was unexpected by history, and in which a thorough post-mortem examination fails to demonstrate an adequate cause for death (Bergman, Beckwith & Ray, 1970).

The following text will review certain epidemiological, pathological and physiological findings related to SIDS as background for the proposed study. For a comprehensive review of SIDS, the reader is referred to these recently published reviews (Brooks, 1982; Kelly & Shannon, 1982; Shannon & Kelly, 1984; Valdes-Dapena, 1980). In addition, as a basis for comparison, developmental findings in normal healthy infants will be included where relevant. Based on this information, an experimental methodology, which could be used as a screening test for detection of infants at risk for SIDS, will be proposed to examine the development

of the normal infant's cardiorespiratory response in the
first year of life.

Epidemiology

Epidemiologic evidence has been gathered by the
scientific community in an effort to identify a population
of infants who might be at increased risk for succumbing to
SIDS. In the absence of pathological evidence which could
directly account for SIDS, the epidemiological findings
also have been instrumental in generating hypotheses about
the etiology of SIDS. It is important that any hypothesis
about the cause of SIDS account for these epidemiological
factors. It has been found that SIDS occurs while the
infant is asleep in the early morning hours, between
midnight and six a.m., with no cry or stridor (Peterson,
1980). The incidence of infant mortality due to SIDS peaks
between two to four months of age. Less than ten percent
of all SIDS deaths occur when infants are younger than two
weeks and older than six months of age (Brooks, 1982). It
should be noted, however, that the peak age for infant
mortality of known causes also occurs at two to four months
of postnatal age (Kelly & Shannon, 1982).

About 60% of SIDS victims are male and incidence for
nonwhites is twice that for whites; SIDS is more
common in low birth weight infants (i.e., 11/1000 live
births), subsequent siblings of SIDS victims (i.e., 21/1000

live births) and in the surviving twin of SIDS victims
(i.e., 42/1000 live births) (Peterson, 1980). These data
suggest that either genetic factors have promoted the
demise of these infants or an environmental influence has
affected their intrauterine or extrauterine development. It
should be noted, however, that no difference was found
between the concordance of SIDS episodes in monozygotic and
dizygotic twin pairs; in addition, the incidence of SIDS in
full first cousins of SIDS victims did not differ from the
incidence in the general population (Peterson, 1980).
Thus, overall the data do not tend to support a genetic
component to SIDS.

There are several epidemiological perinatal-factors
which indicate an environmental influence on SIDS. SIDS
infants are born with higher incidence to young, unmarried
mothers of lower socioeconomic levels who have had poor
prenatal care, have short interpregnancy intervals, have
previous fetal loss and who are smokers or have narcotic
dependency (Valdes-Dapena, 1980). Other environmental
factors which may play a role in SIDS are altitude of
residence and air temperature. Specifically, SIDS incidence
increases as the altitude of residence increases and
the postnatal age of the infant at death decreased with
altitude from a mean of 17 weeks at 300 meters to nine
weeks at 1200 meters (Getts & Hill, 1982). SIDS exhibits a

seasonal variation being more apt to occur during the colder winter months. This has been shown in countries north of the equator peaking between November and March and countries south of the equator peaking between May and September (Moore, 1981; Peterson, 1980; Taylor, 1982). Moreover, a spectral analysis of the SIDS incidence in Los Angeles County from 1974-79 confirmed this seasonal peak of SIDS in addition to revealing the coincidence of decreased air temperature with increases in frequency of SIDS mortality within this period (Hoppenbrouwers & Hodgman, 1982).

On the basis of epidemiologic studies, several groups of infants are believed to be at enhanced risk for SIDS and have been most extensively tested by physiologic studies. They are 1) preterm (i.e., low birth weight) infants with histories of apnea (i.e., cessation of breathing) and bradycardia; 2) infants who have had a near-miss or aborted episode of SIDS, including apnea, cyanosis or pallor and unresponsiveness that responds to intervention of stimulation or resuscitation; and 3) siblings of SIDS infants. There has been some controversy regarding the use of terms like "near-miss" or "aborted" SIDS because they imply with some certainty that the infant almost died when in fact there is no way of knowing whether or not the infant would have spontaneously resumed breathing without assistance (Brooks, 1982). Therefore, the term "Apnea of Infancy" or AI, as suggested by Brooks (1982), will be adopted and used throughout to describe "an unexplained cessation of breathing for 20 seconds or longer, or a shorter respiratory pause associated with bradycardia, cyanosis or pallor." Clearly this term describes a clinical syndrome of respiratory abnormality similar to the sleep apnea of adults or the apnea of prematurity.

Pathology

Report of excessive frequency of prolonged apneic episodes during sleep, in infants who subsequent to their examination died of SIDS, promoted study of the hypothesis that SIDS victims were experiencing recurrent periods of apnea-associated hypoxia prior to their death (Steinschneider, 1972). Among the plethora of hypotheses about the cause of SIDS, most investigatory work in the past decade has centered on the apnea hypothesis (Valdes-Dapena, 1980). A number of post-mortem studies were published shortly after Steinschneider's report which supported the hypothesis that the SIDS is the terminal event in infants who were suffering from a prolonged hypoxic process, which possibly resulted from anomalies in ventilatory control (e.g., Naeye, 1973; 1976). Based on this hypothesis, one would anticipate anomalies in the anatomic sites of ventilatory control (brain stem and carotid body), as well as the organs which are usually affected by chronic hypoxia (the brain, pulmonary vasculature, liver, adrenal glands and periadrenal brown fat).

The main pathological findings have demonstrated that SIDS victims differed from healthy infants who were victims of accidental injury in that SIDS infants had hypertrophic right ventricles in direct proportion to hypertrophy and hyperplasia of pulmonary arteriolar smooth muscle, increased volume of chromaffin cells in the adrenal medulla, retention of periadrenal brown fat and presence of hepatic extramedullary hematopoiesis (Naeye, 1973; Naeye, 1976; Naeye, Whalen, Ryser & Fisher, 1976). Moreover, upon histologic analysis of SIDS cases, Naeye (1976) found increases in brain stem astroglial density, particularly in the midline area of the watershed zone of brain stem circulation. Other recent findings of increased glomic volume of the carotid body in those SIDS victims with evidence of hypertrophy of the pulmonary vasculature have been reported (Naeye, Fisher, Ryser & Whalen, 1976) and reduction of myelinated fibers in the cervical vagus nerve in some SIDS victims (Sachis, Armstrong, Becker & Bryan, 1981).

The finding of increased muscularity and hyperplasia of the pulmonary arteries has been independently described in SIDS victims (Shannon, 1980; Valdes-Dapena, Gillane, Cassady, Catherman & Ross, 1980; Williams, Vawter &

Reid, 1979). These anatomic changes also have been induced in animals exposed to repeated episodes of hypoxia (Rabinovitch, Gamble, Nadas, Meittinen & Reid, 1979) and are typical of children who die after prolonged exposure to the hypoxic conditions of high altitude (Naeye, 1973). The increased hypertrophy of the right ventricle may be a result of the increased pulmonary arteriolar resistance, which forces the heart to pump against a narrower opening. Brown fat and hepatic hematopoiesis normally disappears within the first year of life but its disappearance is delayed in SIDS infants, which is a common finding also noted in autopsy of hypoxic-children residing in high altitude (Naeye et al., 1976). The astroglial proliferation in the brain stem has affected areas such as the nucleus and tractus of solitarius, nucleus ambiguous, raphe nucleus and dorsal vagal nucleus, which are critical in the autonomic control of the cardiovascular and respiratory systems. Similar and more extensive CNS damage has been observed in post-mortem examination of preterm infants with chronic hypoxia due to respiratory distress syndrome (Brand & Bignami, 1969). In addition, perinatal asphyxia for 10-15 minutes in monkeys resulted in a pattern of brain damage which always involved midline brain stem structures (Myers, 1972). Takashima, Armstrong, Becker and Bryan (1978) have postulated that periods of cerebral ischemia may accompany the prolonged periods of apnea and hypoxemia in SIDS infants, which in turn may result in the observed medullary lesions and consequent astroglial proliferation. For this to occur the medullary lesions would have to result from discrete ischemia to brain stem otherwise more widespread damage would be observed.

In sum, a case has been made for the etiology of SIDS, whereby an infant acutely or chronically exposed to hypoxic conditions may develop abnormal cardiorespiratory control due to lesions in the critical brain stem areas. The resultant prolonged periods of apnea or hypoventilation could lead to further hypoxia and establish a positive feedback loop of increasing pathologic tissue damage or at least impaired function in regions of cardiorespiratory control. Eventually, perhaps when challenged, the cardiorespiratory regulatory mechanisms can no longer compensate for the hypoxemic conditions and respiratory failure results.

Cardiorespiratory Physiology

Since post-mortem studies can only provide clues to the etiology of SIDS, physiologic studies have been performed on living infants. What pre-mortem data on SIDS victims are available were derived from studies of infants who have died of SIDS subsequent to physiologic recording. Other than this chance occurrence, there obviously can be no systematic study of the physiologic responses of these infants. However, investigators have studied infants

thought to be at risk for SIDS: infants with AI and
siblings of SIDS victims. They have typically been
contrasted with age-matched, healthy infants. It should
be noted that most studies of SIDS examine the target
physiological response longitudinally over the infant's
development. This is entirely appropriate because the risk
for SIDS seems to be a developmental phenomenon in which
the infant is at increasing risk from birth to 2-4 months
and then with maturation risk declines.

Control of Cardiac Function

Investigations of heart rate (HR) and HR variability
patterns have been performed to determine whether
manifestations of malfunctioning autonomic control
mechanisms could be detected in at-risk infants. During
maternal labor, fetal HR recordings of infants who
subsequently were SIDS victims revealed no differences from
control infants (Hoppenbrouwers, Zanini & Hodgman, 1979).
Siblings of SIDS infants, however, displayed greater fetal
HR variability and more frequent bradycardia than controls
but no difference in overall fetal HR levels when monitored
in-utero while their mothers slept (Hoppenbrouwers,
Hodgman, Harper & Sterman, 1981). The authors suggested
that the increased variability and bradycardic changes in
the siblings may reflect an increased level of intrauterine
hypoxic challenge in the siblings, whereas the effects of
hypoxia may have been concealed by the birthing process in

the SIDS infants. The results in the siblings, however, should be viewed with caution since they are confounded by maternal sleep disturbance, which was higher in mothers of siblings of SIDS than control mothers.

The course of maturation of HR and HR variability for healthy infants has been documented over the first six months of life (Harper, Leake, Hodgman & Hoppenbrouwers, 1982). For HR levels, there is an increase in HR from birth to one month after which rate declines steadily. In contrast, HR was faster in both siblings of SIDS and in AI infants during sleep, displaying a sharper rise and slower decline in the first four months of life (Harper, Leake, Hoppenbrouwers, Sterman, McGinty & Hodgman, 1978; Harper et al., 1982; Leistner, Haddad, Epstein, Lai, Epstein, Eng & Mellins, 1980). These differences were present only in quiet sleep (QS) state (Harper et al., 1982); whereas others observed these differences in both QS and active sleep (AS) state (Leistner et al., 1980). For HR variability in normals, sleep state had a more marked effect. Awake variability was greater than asleep; during sleep, QS was less varible than AS (Harper et al., 1982). Moreover, during QS, HR variability declined rapidly up to one month and then increased rapidly between one and three months after which it became stable. In AS a steady decline in variability was observed over the first six months. In contrast, awake HR variability increased up to two months and then rapidly declined between two and four months after which it stabilized.

No difference has been observed between normals and siblings of SIDS in the maturation of HR variability during sleep up to six months of age, although risk infants displayed reduced variability in the first two months when awake (Harper et al., 1982). On the other hand, others found less HR variability in AI infants than in healthy controls during AS and QS between two and four months (Leistner et al., 1980). Harper and colleagues (1978) have attributed the increased HR levels in the at-risk infants to a reduction in vagal tone. Leistner and colleagues (1980) argue, instead, that the elevated HR levels are due to enhanced sympathoadrenal drive. This is based on the histologic evidence in SIDS victims of hypertrophy of the chromaffin cell layer of the adrenal medulla, which may indicate increased norepinephrine synthesis. Further support of the latter hypothesis was derived from evidence of a shorter Q-T electrocardiographic interval in AI infants than controls over the first four months of life regardless of state, which suggested sympathetic or adrenal mediated enhanced-conduction (Haddad, Epstein, Epstein, Mazza, Mellins & Krongrad, 1979). Although sympathoadrenal mediation may be a possibility for the shortened Q-T interval, ventricular repolarization may also be affected by decreased vagal tone (Prystowsky, Jackman, Rinkenberger, Heger & Zipes, 1981). Regardless of the autonomic mediation, it still remains possible that the elevated HR levels in the at-risk infants represent a compensatory response to hypoxia; the increased cardiac output could act to compensate for the oxygen deficiency.

Control of Respiratory Function

Respiratory patterns. The respiratory rates (RR) of siblings of SIDS have been measured throughout the night across the first six months of age (Hoppenbrouwers, Jenson, Hodgman, Harper & Sterman, 1980). In both normals and siblings, RR declined with increasing age. However, regardless of sleep state, in each age group the RR rate of the SIDS siblings was faster than the control infants, which was interpreted as a compensatory response to hypoxia. Both groups of infants displayed a developmental trend in RR pattern throughout the night. In both AS and transitional sleep (TS), normals and siblings displayed a U-shaped RR pattern throughout the night at all ages. In QS this U-shaped RR pattern did not appear in normals until three months. Siblings, however, displayed this U-shaped pattern prematurely at one month during QS. The authors posit that this was due to a transient acceleration of maturation of the nightly RR pattern in the siblings. Respiratory variability decreased with increasing age in all infants although siblings of SIDS displayed enhanced variability in QS at three months.

In a parallel study of AI infants over the first six months, the data do not entirely replicate these findings (Hodgman, Hoppenbrouwers, Geidel, Hadeed, Sterman, Harper & McGinty, 1982). There was no difference in RR or respiratory variability between AI infants and controls, although the decrease in RR with increasing age was replicated. The only other longitudinal study of AI infants observed faster RR and reduced tidal volume in the AI infants at only one and two months. At three months no differences were observed and at four months AI infants' RR was less than controls (Haddad, Leistner, Lai & Mellins, 1981).

In studies on preterm infants who were presumably hypoxemic, faster HR and RR than term infants has been observed throughout the first six postnatal months, with maximal differences between 2.5 and 3.5 months, the peak period of SIDS vulnerability (Katona, Frasz & Egbert, 1980). It was concluded that since preterm HR and RR maturational patterns were not delayed by the mean difference in post-conceptional age, that both conceptional age and postnatal experience were factors in the development. Therefore, relative to healthy controls all three SIDS risk groups displayed typical patterns of faster

RR over the first six months of life, which could be related to maturational differences and/or compensatory responses to hypoxemia.

Frequency of apnea. There are four types of apnea: central, periodic, obstructive and mixed. Central apnea is defined as a cessation of respiration with no chest or air movement; periodic apnea is also of central origin except that the apnea appears in constellations of short pauses usually greater than three seconds in duration and repeated three or more times with interapnea intervals of 20 seconds or less; obstructive apnea is a disruption in ventilation consisting of a lack of air flow but continued respiratory movements; mixed apnea is initially a central apnea but towards the end of the apneic episode some chest movements appear with no air flow indicating some obstruction (Kelly & Shannon, 1982).

Apnea with duration less than nine seconds is a common finding in healthy infants over the first six months of life (Hoppenbrouwers, Hodgman, Arakawa, Harper & Sterman, 1980). In this study short apnea (2-5 seconds) was more abundant than longer apnea (6-9 seconds) and the incidence of short apnea increased with age while longer apnea incidence decreased with age. It was speculated that this increase with age could probably be accounted for by the same mechanism which was responsible for the concomitant

increase in interbreath interval. The frequency of apnea
longer than ten seconds was common only in the first week
when incidence of all apnea types was greatest. Otherwise,
prolonged apneic episodes were infrequent. Additionally,
sleep state affected apnea frequency, with more apnea
observed in AS than QS. When apnea does occur it has been
found to be of greater duration in QS than AS (Mellins &
Haddad, 1983).

There are conflicting data on whether the incidence of
apnea is enhanced in at-risk infants. In the fourteen
years since Steinschneider (1972) reported his findings of
prolonged and excessive apnea in infants who subsequently
died of SIDS, a number of studies have also reported
increased incidence of apnea in infants at risk for SIDS.
In another study, Steinschneider (1977) observed longer and
more frequent central apnea as well as increased frequency
of periodic apnea in infants with AI. However, apnea
shorter than 20 seconds was not examined. An increase in
frequency and duration of periodic apnea in both siblings of
SIDS and AI infants has also been reported (Kelly &
Shannon, 1979; Kelly, Walker, Cahen & Shannon, 1980).

In contrast, Guilleminault and colleagues have observed
no significant differences between AI infants and controls in
incidence of periodic apnea or in central apnea greater
than ten seconds (Guilleminault, Ariagno, Korobkin, Nagel,

Baldwin, Coons & Owen, 1979; Guilleminault et al., 1981).

However, they did report an increase in short (i.e., three

to ten seconds) mixed and obstructive apnea frequency in AI

infants from three weeks to four months of age.

Unfortunately, they failed to report or analyze data on

central apneas less than ten seconds. They report the

means of their 1979 study for central apneas from three to

ten seconds in a more recent publication but failed again

to analyse them (Guilleminault, Souquet, Ariagno, Korobkin

& Simmons, 1984). Inspection of these means suggested that

these short central apneas were more frequent than the

combined mixed and obstructive frequencies of similar

duration. In addition, it appeared that the AI infants

had a greater incidence of short central apneas at three

and six weeks of age but not at twelve weeks.

Additional contradictions were evident in other

research. Greater incidence of short apneas in subsequent

siblings of SIDS than controls was observed only when in AS

at two weeks of age (Kelly, Twanmoh & Shannon, 1982). No

difference in these infants was observed at eight and

fourteen weeks of age. Some researchers report no

difference in the frequency or duration of respiratory

pauses in AI and control infants (Mellins & Haddad, 1983).

Conversely, other researchers have found a reduced

incidence of central apnea in siblings of SIDS than in

controls in AS and QS (Hoppenbrouwers, Hodgman, McGinty, Harper & Sterman, 1980). In this study, the incidence of mixed and obstructive apnea and central apnea greater than ten seconds was too low to analyse. However, it was found that from one week to six months of age, differences between infant groups were greatest for short apneas of two to five seconds in QS; whereas for longer apneas of six to nine seconds differences were greatest in AS and TS. In another study, using AI and normal infants from one week to six months of age, this same laboratory reported no differences in periodic, mixed, obstructive or central apnea frequency (Hodgman et al., 1982). However, although the trends were nonsignificant, AI infants did display lower frequency of short and longer central apnea in this study.

In summary, both the Shannon and Guilleminault research groups report excessive incidence of apnea in infants at risk for SIDS, although they don't agree on which type of apnea is significant. Shannon claims that its periodic apnea that is excessive and Guilleminault emphasizes mixed and obstructive apneas. Alternatively, the Haddad group reports no difference in apnea frequency and the Hoppenbrouwers group found frequency reductions in central apneic episodes less than ten seconds in duration. Guilleminault and colleagues have recently emphasized that

because of differences in study design, definition of AI,
subject age, time and duration of study, recorded
measurements, analysis of respiratory events, and setting
of session, it is difficult to compare between laboratory
studies (Guilleminault, Ariagno, Korobkin, Coons, Owen-
Boeddiker & Baldwin, 1981). The lack of standardization
may therefore be responsible for the differences or lack
thereof in apnea frequency between studies. It seems clear
from the review above that there has been little
interlaboratory replication and although there may be
differences one way or another in the frequency of a
certain type of apnea, these are restricted to the
particular circumstances of measurement. Hence, the role
of apnea in SIDS remains equivocal.

The finding of an increase or decrease in apnea
incidence has been posited to relate to defective
respiratory control interacting with a myriad of potential
factors such as sleep state and CNS maturation (Shannon &
Kelly, 1982). The lack of consistent replicable finding
suggests that the apnea is of varied origin and probably
constitutes only one of the many triggering stimuli in SIDS
infants. Based upon the reported rates of apnea in the
above studies, it can be calculated that the risk groups
spent approximately only one minute per hour in apnea
(McGinty & Sterman, 1980). At this level the frequency of

apnea can hardly be considered a significant factor in the induction of hypoxic conditions in risk infants. Apnea may only represent the final common pathway in a series of events preceding death.

Control of ventilation. There is evidence that the mechanisms which control breathing begin to mature and respond to respiratory stimuli such as level of carbon dioxide and metabolic acidosis during fetal development. For a review of the ontogeny of fetal respiratory development see Maloney and Bowes (1983). The fetus stops initiating breathing when the partial pressure of arterial oxygen (PaO_2) is lowered to about 15 mmHg (Wilds, 1978). The adult, however, increases ventilation when PaO_2 is lowered below 50 mmHg (Dejours, 1963). The adult's hyperpnea or ventilatory increase is sustained until normoxic levels are achieved. The newborns' response to a 5% decrement in inspired oxygen differs from that of both the fetus and the adult (Rigatto, 1977). In the newborn, hypoxia induces a biphasic compensatory response: an initial ventilatory increase within the first two minutes followed by a decrement to and below baseline ventilatory levels. The newly-born preterm infant at 33 and 37 weeks gestation responds the same as the newborn (Rigatto, 1982). Therefore, gestational age does not seem to be a factor. However, postnatal maturation may play a role, since the initial ventilatory increase in the preterm becomes larger with postnatal age and the adult-like sustained hyperpnea to hypoxia begins about one month after birth (Rigatto, 1982). Full term infants, on the other hand, begin sustained hypoxia-induced hyperpnea at about two weeks of postnatal age (Rigatto, 1977). The progressive increase in ventilation seen in the preterm infants suggests that maturational changes occurred in either respiratory pump mechanics or peripheral chemoreception, or both.

The initial increase in ventilation has been attributed to stimulation of the peripheral chemoreceptors because of the rapidity of the ventilatory response to hypoxia onset (Rigatto, 1982). The subsequent fall in ventilation has been postulated to be due to adjustments in pulmonary mechanics (e.g., lung compliance decrease), central depression of respiratory drive, and immature interaction between carotid sinus chemoreceptive afferent feedback and the central respiratory mechanisms (Haddad, Schaeffer & Bazzy, 1983). Hence, it was suggested that in infants at-risk for SIDS hypoxic depression in an immature CNS could induce an imbalance of excitatory and inhibitory influences, which may supercede the chemoreceptor effect on breathing. This could result in a state of chronic hypoventilation or be manifested by a noncompensatory decrement in ventilation to an acute hypoxic challenge.

Current data suggest that, when compared with adults, infants have a reduced PaO_2, indicating that infants are normally exposed to a hypoxic challenge (Brooks, Schluete, Nabelet & Tooley, 1978). More systematic study of this hypoxic stimulus revealed that periodic apnea could be induced in preterm infants when subjecting them to mild hypoxia (Rigatto, 1982). After prolonged exposure, however, incidence of periodic apnea decreased and central apnea increased during the decreased ventilation of the secondary limb of the biphasic response. This suggested that hypoxia may be an important triggering stimulus for apnea when the respiratory system is depressed in immature nervous systems. A similar finding was observed in AI infants exposed to a 3% decrease in oxygen; most notably, however, these at-risk infants displayed greater incidence of periodic apnea and central apnea to this hypoxic stimulus than did the control infants (Brady, Ariagno, Watts, Goldman & Dumpit, 1978).

There have been numerous reports of periods of prolonged apnea in infants at-risk for SIDS (Shannon, Kelly & O'Connell, 1977; Steinschneider, 1977; Kaun, Blum, Engleman & Waterschoot, 1982). Increased durations of apnea in AI infants have been associated with corresponding greater reductions in the transcutaneous partial pressure of oxygen ($tcPO_2$), which is a noninvasive measure of PaO_2 (Kaun et al., 1982). The prolonged duration of apnea in the AI infants could be related to a higher peripheral or central chemoreceptor response threshold to hypoxia or hypercapnia. That is, during apnea greater hypoxic and/or hypercapnic levels are accumulated before respiration is initiated resulting in prolonged apneic episodes. Therefore, it would be expected that infants with this elevated threshold would be sluggish to respond to a hypoxic or hypercapnic challenge.

Support for this suggestion comes from studies of ventilatory response to hypoxic and hypercapnic stimuli in at-risk infants. Impaired ventilatory increases to a 5% reduction in inspired oxygen (i.e., 15% oxygen) were observed in AI infants (Hunt, McCulloch & Brouillette, 1981). Also, blunted ventilatory responses and a more pronounced subsequent depression of ventilation were observed in AI infants to hypoxic challenges of 15% oxygen compared to controls (Haidmayer, Kurz, Kenner, Wurm & Pfeiffer, 1982). Concomitant with the depression in ventilation, were more pronounced and rapid declines in $tcPO_2$ values in the AI infants. Moreover, other studies have found that AI infants displayed less ventilatory response to hypercapnic challenges of 4-5% carbon dioxide than controls (Hajdmayer et al., 1982; Hunt et al., 1981; Marotta, Fort, Mondestin, Hiatt & Hegyi, 1984; Shannon et al., 1977). Therefore, infants at risk for SIDS have reduced hypoxic and hypercapnic ventilatory responses, suggesting reduced sensitivity to chemoreceptive challenge.

In summary, the majority of evidence from cardiorespiratory physiologic investigations has revealed that infants at-risk for SIDS display elevated HR levels and reduced HR variability; RR is also elevated and these infants exhibit a transient acceleration in the developmental pattern of RR while sleeping. There are conflicting data on which type of apnea is present in these infants and whether the frequency of apnea during sleep is excessive or diminished. However, when apnea does occur, the duration is more prolonged and is associated with corresponding decrement in PaO_2. When breathing gas mixtures of decreased oxygen content or increased carbon dioxide content, at-risk infants initially displayed a sluggish ventilatory increase and with prolonged exposure, subsequently exhibited more pronounced depression of ventilation.

Sleep and Breathing

The finding that SIDS infants are typically found dead in the early morning hours, when they were presumed to be asleep, has led some to speculate that sleep precipitates the events leading to SIDS (McGinty & Sterman, 1980). There are rapid maturational changes in sleep and respiratory physiology in the first six months of life. (See Berg and Berg (1979) for a review of the ontogeny of sleep, cardiorespiratory physiology and sensory function in infancy.) During this time, the sleep states become well defined and become more organized within the sleeping periods. There is a consolidation of sleep and waking into longer and longer uninterrupted periods. By four to six months, these become coupled so that the longest of the sleeping periods follows the longest of the waking periods (Coons & Guilleminault, 1982). By three months stereotypic elements of adult electroencephalographic (EEG) sleep patterns can be used to discriminate between AS and QS and stages within QS (Coons & Guileminault, 1982). For a recent comprehensive review of the neurophysiology of sleep the reader may refer to McGinty and Beahm (1984).

In QS breathing is very regular and inspiration is prolonged. It has been suggested that during QS the forebrain and the brain stem are uncoupled (Harper, 1983). However, slow-rhythmic descending discharges from regions of the forebrain have been documented, which may be pacing the lower brain stem structures in QS (Harper & Sieck, 1980). Other forebrain areas have been implicated in the gating of QS onset (Harper, 1983). The influence of the forebrain in the ontogeny of QS may be evidenced by the observation of the emergence of a dramatic postnatal increase in the proportion of total sleep time spent in QS associated with concomitant increases in postnatal forebrain development (Parmalee, Stern & Harris, 1972).

During AS, breathing is extremely variable and RR is increased; desynchronous descending influences of the forebrain and other areas on brain stem respiratory and motor neurons affect rhythm and rate of breathing and also diminish muscle tone (Schulte, Albani, Schmizer & Bentele, 1982). Phasic bursts of rapid eye movement and twitches in the limbs and peripheral musculature occur. The rib cage loses stability and during inspiration paradoxical deflation of the rib cage may be observed due to depression of intercostal and abdominal muscle activity (Henderson-Smart & Read, 1978). This might indicate that AS represents the state of greatest vulnerability to apnea and hypoxia. However, other observations indicate that AS may be associated with improved breathing. For example, oxygen level in the blood of infants is improved in AS compared to QS (Brooks et al., 1978).

There is evidence accumulating that the state of greatest vulnerability for apneic episode may be QS. When kittens were chronically exposed to hypoxic conditions, 28%

of them failed to compensate in QS and exhibited hypoventilation and prolonged apnea, in some cases progressing to death; in AS the hypoxemic conditions in these animals were transiently reversed with faster RR and decreased incidence of apnea (McGinty & Sterman, 1980). This evidence suggests that the conflicting reports of apnea incidence in the at-risk infants may reflect differential sampling of infants who may or may not be capable of producing compensatory cardiorespiratory responses. In support of this possibility, it may be recalled that the compensatory pattern of elevated HR and RR with reduced incidence of apnea (which was more pronounced in QS) was observed in siblings of SIDS who, by definition, had had a healthy neonatal course with no documented prolonged apnea attack (Hoppenbrouwers et al., 1980); whereas no compensatory pattern was observed in AI infants who had a prior history of prolonged apnea (Hodgman et al., 1982). This suggests that the siblings of SIDS may differ from the AI infants in the ability to compensate with increased cardiac output and ventilation to a hypoxic challenge; whereas the AI infants having previously demonstrated some pathophysiologic disorder by virtue of their prolonged apneic attack, may no longer be capable of producing compensatory cardiorespiratory responses.

Other evidence suggests some alteration in the maturation of sleep physiology in at-risk infants. Siblings of SIDS victims display an accelerated maturation of 12-15 Hz EEG activity in QS and 4-7 Hz EEG activity in AS between one and two months of age (Sterman, Harper, Hoppenbrouwers, McGinty & Hodgman, 1979). It was suggested that an abnormal stimulus such as hypoxia may have caused this transient acceleration in EEG development. It has been speculated that an accelerated maturation of the forebrain inhibitory influences on medullary respiratory centers may be present in these infants (Hoppenbrouwers & Hodgman, 1982). Other evidence indicates that, rather than being accelerated, the sleep state development in at-risk infants is delayed. The percent time in QS was less in AI infants than in controls at three and four months of age, suggesting a maturational delay or disturbance in the AI infants (Haddad, Walsh, Leistner, Grodin & Mellins, 1981). Analysis of the temporal sequencing of sleep-wake epochs in normal infants and siblings of SIDS, revealed disturbed patterns of state organization at two to three months of age (Harper, Frostig, Taube, Hoppenbrouwers & Hodgman, 1983). Siblings were observed to have longer intervals between periods of wakefulness, a shorter mean QS cycle period and an increase in the frequency of state transitions. The prolonged periods of uninterrupted sleep may reflect an inability to arouse from sleep (Harper et al., 1983). Hunt (1981) observed that AI infants also showed a tendency to remain asleep in the face of hypoxic challenge; whereas control infants displayed an increased frequency of arousal from sleep when inspired oxygen was progressively decreased to 15%. The authors posited that the failure to arouse may be due to a defect in peripheral chemoreceptor sensitivity. Others have hypothesized that the chronic hypoxemia of SIDS, and the hypoventilation and failure to arouse in at-risk infants may be due to tonic overactive synthesis of endorphins, which have previously been associated with the CNS suppression of respiration and wakefulness (Kuich & Zimmerman, 1981). Some support for this theory was observed in post-mortem examination of met-enkephalin (an endogenous endorphin) levels in cerebrospinal fluid, when it was found that SIDS victims had greater concentrations than age-matched controls (Rappaport, Kozakewich, Fenton, Mandell, Vawter & Yang, 1984). Regardless of the etiology, the failure to make transition from sleep to waking may place these infants at greater risk. The finding of increased incidence of apnea, occurring antecedent to awakening in infants in the first six months of life, suggests that arousal from sleep may be an important mechanism in terminating apneic episodes (Guilleminault et al., 1981).

Cardiorespiratory Responses to Airstream Stimulation

The evidence from pathological and physiologic investigations indicate that infants at-risk for SIDS may be chronically hypoxic, are sluggish to respond to hypoxic and hypercapnic stimuli with a ventilatory increase and are less likely to arouse from sleep during such a challenge; also, while asleep they consistently exhibit prolonged periods of apnea with concomitant bradycardia. Hence one of the most striking deficits in these infants is their higher tolerance of hypoxia and hypercapnea before responding appropriately. This deficit is particularly apparent from two to four months of age, which is the period of most rapid CNS development and also the age of greatest vulnerability for SIDS. Therefore it may be possible to detect an infant at risk for SIDS by eliciting apnea and thereby establishing a hypoxic or hypercapnic challenge to which they would be expected to respond sluggishly. The prolonged apneic episodes that are spontaneously produced by these infants are probably related to a more general CNS dysfunction of autonomic depressor reflexes involving the complex interactions of the medullary chemoreceptors with inputs from the trigeminal, glossopharyngeal and vagus cranial nerves, peripheral chemoreceptors, sleep control mechanisms and cardiorespiratory regulating mechanisms.

Investigations in infants of the ontogeny of reflex mechanisms which when stimulated can induce apnea are limited to four areas of research: 1) laryngeal chemoreceptor stimulation and gastroesophageal reflux; 2) ventilatory response to hypoxic and hypercapnic exposure; 3) vagal-mediated reflexes in compensation to inspiratory load; and 4) dive reflex and facial cooling with an airstream.

In animals stimulation of the laryngeal chemoreceptors with chemical irritants have been found to evoke prolonged apnea (Downing & Lee, 1975). There has been a report of an association of apnea and gastroesophageal reflux in premature infants, which presumably induces reflex apnea by acidic reflux stimulation of the laryngeal chemoreceptors (Herbst, Minton & Book, 1979). However, others have found no such relationship in premature and full-term infants, and AI infants (Ariagno, Guilleminault, Baldwin & Owen-Boeddiker, 1982; Walsh, Farrell, Keenan, Lucas & Kramer, 1981). Some have studied hypercapnic ventilatory responsiveness and sustained hypoxic hyperpnea and have observed that at some critical level of PaO_2 and $PaCO_2$ periodic apnea is induced and with further exposure central apnea eventually occurs (e.g., Rigatto, 1982). However, the role of this mechanism in initiating prolonged apnea has not been examined. Inflation of infants lungs in order

to activate vagal-inhibition of respiration has revealed
that premature infants are more susceptible to respiratory
inhibition than full-term healthy infants at any age (e.g.,
Boychuk, Rigatto & Sheshia, 1977; Kirkpatrick, Olinsky,
Bryan & Bryan, 1976). Although this technique when studied
developmentally would provide information on the ontogeny
of vagal reflexes in compensation to an inspiratory load,
it is subject to confounding influences of changes in
pulmonary mechanics due to sleep state (Henderson-Smart,
1984). Nevertheless, this test is more likely to provide
information on inspiratory load compensation than
information on the development of mechanisms of prolonged
respiratory cessation. Although research on these first
three areas could be of importance to a better understanding
of apneic episodes in SIDS, apnea induction by the dive
reflex and facial cooling may have the greatest relevance.

The dive reflex is a depressor reflex which appears to
resemble the acute cardiorespiratory response observed in
infants during an apneic episode. Diving in animals like
seals elicits apnea, profound bradycardia and peripheral
vasoconstriction. These responses have the clear
physiological function of conserving oxygen by reducing
circulation to tissues of greater anaerobic capacity (e.g.,
skin, mesentary, muscle) and providing circulation to
tissues less tolerant of the effects of oxygen deprivation

(e.g., heart, brain). The ophthalmic division of the trigeminal nerve, which in humans innervates the forehead, eyelids and dorsum of the nose, was found to be primarily responsible for completing the afferent pathway by which dive reflexes were elicited in the duck (Anderson, 1963).

The dive reflex has also been observed in humans (e.g., Elsner, Franklin, Van Citters & Kenney, 1966; Kawakami, Natelson & DuBois, 1967). More recently, elaboration of the relevant eliciting stimuli has revealed that mere submersion of the face in cold water was sufficient to elicit the bradycardia and peripheral vasoconstriction typical of the dive reflex (Hurwitz & Furedy, 1979). Furthermore, it was the combination of cold facial stimuli and breath holding that produced greater bradycardia and vasoconstriction than in either control conditions of face immersion (while breathing through a snorkel) or breath holding alone. Others have found that the dive reflex was even more pronounced with colder water temperatures (Furedy, Morrison, Heslegrave & Arabian, 1983; Song, Lee, Chung & Hong, 1969). The dive reflex literature illustrates the significance of cold facial stimulation in effecting cardiovascular and respiratory responses.

In human infants apneic and bradycardic responses have been elicited by nasopharyngeal suction and by blowing oxygen over the infants' face (Brown, Ostheimer, Bell &

Datta, 1976; Cordero & Hon, 1971). Both of these procedures are currently used to aid in establishing respiration during delivery of the newborn (Gregory, 1975). Cardiac rate changes were elicited by abdominal and nasal airstream stimulation in infants from the first day to the fifth postnatal month (Allen, Howard, Smith, McCubbin & Weaver, 1979; Lipton, Steinschneider & Richmond, 1966). In both of these studies of healthy full term infants it was reported that the predominant response to airstream stimulation in both locations was a transient HR acceleration. No respiratory measures were reported.

Others have examined the cardiorespiratory responses during sleep in two day to four month-old infants with AI and normal infants in response to a two-second airstream stimulus directed to the nasal passages (McCubbin, Smith, Allen, Wood & McGraw, 1977). They observed greater magnitude of bradycardic response to the airstream stimulation in AI infants. No explanation was given for the apparently contradictory finding of deceleration in response to the facial airstream in this study as compared with acceleration in previous studies. Perhaps this discrepant finding was due to the peak-drop cardiac measure they employed, which was biased in favor of detecting decelerations by sampling the lowest HR achieved post-stimulus onset. In addition, they did not examine the topography of the HR response from stimulus onset, which would have provided more information on the temporal effect of the stimulus and would have been a less biased measure. Brief apneic episodes in response to the airstream stimulus were observed but no difference in apnea duration existed between the two infant groups. Unfortunately, no further attempt was made to examine the apnea responses quantitatively. Moreover, no systematic analysis was performed to partial out the effects of sleep state, postnatal age or presence or absence of apnea from their possible effects on the cardiorespiratory responses observed.

The proposed study, herein, was designed to establish the normative response to facial airstream stimulation in infants throughout the first year of life. This study has a focus similar to that of McCubbin et al. (1977) but utilized a more systematic design, including the appropriate control conditions to compare the cardiorespiratory responses. The study was designed to assess in sleeping infants developmental changes in cardiorespiratory responses to airstream stimulation in the first year of life by 1) determining whether airstream stimulation of the facial region supplied by the ophthalmic branch of the trigeminal nerve (i.e., forehead, eyelids and dorsum of the nose) would elicit apnea more frequently than a control airstream stimulus directed to the abdomen (i.e., rostral to the umbilicus); 2) measuring the HR response on a second-by-second basis and average a sufficiently large number of homogeneous trials to determine the precise topography of the cardiac response to airstream stimulation; and 3) examining the effect of apnea elicited by the airstream stimulus on the HR response topography.

This study will be informative for the following reasons. First, the examination of the cardiorespiratory responses to repeated airstream stimulation will provide information on the maturation of cardiorespiratory control in the production of depressor reflexes in normal infants cross-sectionally throughout the first year of life. It will be informative to determine whether the cardio-respiratory responses in infants, during the period of most rapid CNS development (i.e., two to four months of age) and vulnerability to SIDS, differ from responses during earlier or later postnatal age. Second, it will provide more information on the cardiorespiratory effects of conditions of facial cooling similar to those which exist presently in hospital delivery protocol manipulations such as nasopharyngeal suction and oxygen blown over the face. Third, since the airstream stimulus is not substantially different from that which the infant might commonly experience in every day life, this study may shed some light on the eliciting conditions of apnea and bradycardia in normal healthy infants. Fourth, this simple reflex test of the integrity of trigeminal-brainstem-cardiorespiratory function could have prognostic significance for screening of cardiorespiratory risk for SIDS. However, baseline data in a normative sample are required initially so that the results of this study will provide information against which data from high risk infants may be compared.

CHAPTER 2
METHODS

Subjects

Eighty-nine infants participated in this study. Infants were recruited from three postnatal age groups: newborn, 2-4 months and 8-12 months. The criteria for selection were 1) full term gestational age of 38-42 weeks; 2) an uneventful maternal and obstetrical history; 3) uncomplicated spontaneous vaginal delivery and neonatal course; 4) physically healthy at the time of testing with no respiratory infection and with no medication being used; 5) five minute APGAR score of greater than or equal to seven. Subjects were not included in the sample if they did not fulfill these criteria or if they failed to remain asleep for at least ten of twenty possible trials. Of the 89 infants recorded in the testing situation, 37 were eliminated for the following reasons: other than a spontaneous vaginal delivery (n=16); failed to remain asleep (n=13); respiratory infection at time of testing (n=3); premature at birth (n=3); experimenter error (n=2). There were 14 newborn (NB) subjects, 23 2-4 month subjects and 15 8-12 month subjects who satisfied these criteria.

Maternal and infant hospital medical records of the newborn group were surveyed to insure that all criteria were met. For the older groups information on the infants' delivery and neonatal course and the maternal obstetrical history was obtained in a questionaire during testing (see Appendix A). Table 1, 2 and 3, respectively, shows the sex, gestational age (GA), postnatal age (PNA) at the time of testing, birth weight (BW), APGAR scores, race (R), maternal age (MA), and maternal medication (MED) at delivery for each infant in the three age groups included in this study.

Newborn subjects were recruited by obtaining permission from their mother or father in the neonatology ward of the J. Hillis Miller Health Center. These subjects received no remuneration for their participation. The older subjects were recruited through the mail. Names of infants born in the appropriate age group were obtained through the Alachua County Health Department. Parents were sent a general letter describing the study and were requested to indicate whether they were interested in participating in the study on an enclosed stamped-postcard. Those parents responding affirmatively were telephoned to schedule an appointment for testing. In this conversation parents were informed about the purpose and specifics of the study and an appointment was scheduled at a time that would correspond to the infant's nap schedule. These subjects received five dollars for their participation.[1]

TABLE 1
Description of the Newborn Subject Pool (Abbreviations used
are as follows: GA is gestational age, PNA is postnatal age,
BW is birth weight, R is race, MA is maternal age, MED is
maternal medication and SEQ is stimulus sequence.)

Subj. No.	Sex	GA (wk)	PNA (hr)	BW (gm)	APGAR 1	5	R	MA (yr)	MED	SEQ
101	F	39	10.5	3740	7	9	C	35	N	A
102	F	40	8.5	2600	9	9	B	20	Y(S & Ph*)	A
103	F	40	12.0	2690	7	8	B	21	Y(S & Ph)	A
104	M	40	16.5	2960	9	9	C	24	N	B
106	M	40	22.5	3140	9	9	B	22	N	A
108	M	41	17.0	3420	9	10	C	19	N	B
109	F	41	25.5	3760	9	9	B	19	N	A
110	F	40	11.0	3440	9	9	B	29	Y(S & Ph)	B
112	F	38	8.0	2800	9	9	B	27	N	A
113	F	40	15.5	2820	6	9	B	19	N	B
114	M	40	11.5	3770	9	9	B	20	N#	B
115	F	39	21.0	3120	9	9	B	17	Y(E#)	B
116	M	41	9.0	3110	9	9	C	17	Y(S & Ph)	B
117	M	38	21.0	3530	8	10	C	23	N	A
Mean		39.8	15.0	3207.1	8.4	9.1		22.3		
Freq.	F 8						B 9		N 9	A 7
	M 6						C 5		Y 5	B 7

* S & Ph denotes stadol and phenergen i.v.
# E denotes epidural

TABLE 2

Description of 2-4 Month-Old Subject Pool (Abbreviations used are as follows: GA is gestational age, PNA is postnatal age, BW is birth weight, R is race, MA is maternal age, MED is maternal medication and SEQ is stimulus sequence.)

Subj. No.	Sex	GA (wk)	PNA (day)	BW (gm)	APGAR 1	APGAR 5	R	MA (yr)	MED	SEQ
201	M	40	74	3610	10	10	C	26	Y(E$^{\#}$ & Ph*)	A
202	F	40	69	3813	8	9	C	35	Y(D**)	A
206	M	39	73	4082	7	10	C	31	Y(D & P$^{@}$)	B
207	M	41	73	2920	9	10	C	25	Y(E)	B
209	F	40	57	3643	–	–	C	26	N	B
210	M	40	53	3572	9	10	C	37	N	B
211	M	40	88	3841	9	9	C	25	N	A
212	M	40	86	3402	9	10	C	23	Y(D & NO$^{\#\#}$)	A
214	M	41	86	3601	–	–	C	30	Y(E & D)	A
216	F	41	44	3898	8	9	C	22	Y(D)	A
218	M	40	62	3317	9	10	C	33	Y(D & Ph)	B
220	F	40	47	3997	9	9	C	31	N	B
225	F	40	74	3544	9	10	C	32	N	B
228	M	40	108	3560	9	9	C	26	Y(D & Ph)	A
231	F	40	65	4100	9	9	C	36	N	A
232	M	40	66	3360	8	9	C	23	N	A
235	F	39	67	3997	6	8	C	27	N	A
236	M	39	86	3090	–	–	C	22	N	A
237	F	40	89	4020	9	10	C	25	N	A
238	F	40	75	3104	9	10	C	22	Y(E)	A
242	M	40	110	3473	9	10	C	42	N	B
243	M	39	55	3515	–	–	C	28	N	B
244	M	40	93	3600	–	–	C	23	N	B
Mean		40.0	73.9	3611.3	8.6	9.5		28.3		
Freq.	F 9						C 23		N 13	A 13
	M 14								Y 10	B 10

* Ph denotes phenergen i.v.
**D denotes demoral i.v.
E denotes epidural
##NO denotes nitrous oxide
@ P denotes pitocin i.v.

TABLE 3

Description of the 8-12 Month-Old Subject Pool (Abbreviations used are as follows: GA is gestational age, PNA is postnatal age, BW is birth weight, R is race, MA is maternal age, MED is maternal medication and SEQ is stimulus sequence.)

Subj. No.	Sex	GA (wk)	PNA (day)	BW (gm)	APGAR 1	APGAR 5	R	MA (yr)	MED	SEQ
304	M	41	256	3374	9	10	C	30	Y(E#)	A
305	F	40	288	3969	8	9	C	33	N	B
306	F	40	312	3730	9	10	C	21	N	A
307	M	39	288	3969	9	10	C	30	N	B
308	M	39	328	3204	9	10	C	27	N	A
312	M	38	243	3062	9	10	C	26	N	A
313	F	42	247	3005	9	10	C	23	N	A
314	M	39	298	3799	7	9	C	28	Y(D**& P@)	B
315	M	40	239	3544	10	10	C	25	N	A
318	M	41	258	3657	8	9	C	27	Y(D & NO##)	A
319	F	41	247	3147	8	10	C	28	Y(E)	B
320	M	39	249	3572	9	10	C	23	Y(E)	B
321	M	41	243	3969	8	9	C	29	Y(E)	A
325	F	40	238	4012	9	10	C	35	N	A
326	F	39	248	3232	7	9	C	18	N	B
Mean		39.9	265.5	3549.7	8.5	9.7		26.9		
Freq.	F 6						C 15		N 9	A 9
	M 9								Y 6	B 6

** D denotes demoral i.v.
# E denotes epidural
NO denotes nitrous oxide
@ P denotes pitocin i.v.

Apparatus

Newborn subjects were tested in a sound-attenuated chamber in a room located next to the NICU, on the third floor, in the J. Hillis Miller Health Center. The door to the chamber was always closed during testing thus separating the subject from the equipment. All these subjects were tested while laying in a 70 X 34 X 27 cm basinette. A 30 X 25 cm opening on the anterior side of the basinette had been made to permit ready access for handling the infant and also permitted an unobstructed avenue for the direction of the stimulus toward the infant. Subjects were continuously monitored by an experimenter in the chamber and could be observed by another experimenter through a window located in the side of the chamber.

All testing of the older infants was done in a small sound-attenuating chamber, which was located in the Psychology building in a separate room from all the equipment, except the equipment responsible for the airstream stimulus. The air delivery equipment had to remain within the testing room just external to the chamber so that the specific dimensions of the air tube and air pressure regulation requirements remained identical between testing locations. This insured that all qualitative and quantitaive aspects of the the airstream would be equivalent between testing locations. The door to the room was always closed during testing but the door to the chamber was always open. All these subjects were tested while laying on a 89 X 54 cm foam-rubber mattress. Subjects were continuously monitored by the experimenter in the room and could be viewed at all times on closed-circuit television by their parent(s) and the other experimenter.

Stimulus onset, duration and minimum intertrial intervals were controlled by an Apple II computer at the newborn laboratory, while an Iconix (6010) clock and relays served this function in the psychology laboratory. Airstream stimuli were produced by electronically opening a solenoid valve fitted on a pressure-regulated scuba tank. The air was directed through a plastic tubing which was 309.9 cm long and had an interior diameter of 4.25 mm. The air tube was freely mobile so that the experimenter could direct the airstream toward either the face or the abdomen without disturbing the infant. For all infants the opening of the air tube was positioned about 8 cm from the skin surface. The intensity of the airpuff was measured by connecting a manometer from a blood pressure sphygmo-manometer (Abco #HR18104-390102) to the end of the air tube. Puff intensities were controlled by adjusting an KGM Equipment Co., regulator (#1208) so that the intensity was about 55 mmHg, which corresponded to 1.06 psi (i.e., 55mmHg = 7,333 $N/(m^2)$ = 1.06 psi). At this level

the airstream was of quite moderate intensity and not
disturbing.

To measure heart rate (HR), the electrocardiogram (EKG)
was recorded from the body surface by silver/silver chloride
11 mm cup electrodes (#650437) containing Synapse
electrolytic paste (Med-Tek Corporation). The two recording
electrodes were placed, respectively, about one cm above the
left nipple and the other on the left side of the rib cage at
chest lead V_6; the grounding electrode was placed on the side
opposite to the former recording electrode. The resultant
electrophysiological signal was recorded on a Narco Bio-
systems physiograph (Model DMP-4B) in the newborn
laboratory and a Beckman Dynograph (Model R411) in the
psychology laboratory and transmitted to yield HR through a
biotachometer on a second channel. Time constants and high
frequency filtering were as follows; for both polygraphs
the high frequency filters were set at 30 Hz while the time
constant was set at .03 seconds. EKG was also recorded on
a Hewlett-Packard (Model 3960) Instrumentation FM tape
recorder in the psychology laboratory and a Teac (Model #A-
2300SX) tape recorder in the newborn laboratory.

Two other measures were recorded polygraphically only.
Respiration was obtained in all subjects by taping a
mercury-filled strain gauge to the abdomen to allow
recording of diaphragmatic excursions. Nasal respiration

was obtained by taping a Narco Bio-systems Thermistor Respiration Transducer (Model #15-077-8) to the infants' upper lip so that the thermistor lay just posterior to one of the nasal openings. Some infants were bothered by this device, which was attached after they fell asleep, so although it was used for all the NB subjects, nasal respiration was monitored for only 13 2-4 month subjects and no 8-12 month subjects. An additional polygraph channel served as an event marker recording the onset and offset of the airstream stimulus. Both polygraphs were run at a paper speed of 10 mm per second.

Experimental Manipulations and Design

The present experiment compared one control condition, abdominal airstream stimulation with the experimental facial airstream stimulation condition. To increase precision and control for individual differences, this two-level conditions factor was varied within subjects and presented in one of two random orders; about half the subjects in each age group received each order. See Appendix B, which includes a listing of the trials and the corresponding schedule for stimulus delivery for each sequence. Each sequence was derived from the random number tables with the stipulation that there be ten trials in each condition, but a given condition could not be repeated more than twice consecutively. Since data were lost due to movement artifact and state change any subject with less than a minimum of five trials of usable data per condition was eliminated from the subject pool. For each subject, data for usable trials were averaged within each condition prior to statistical analyses, thus eliminating a trials factor from subsequent evaluations. In addition, a between-subject factor was introduced by testing subjects cross-sectionally at three postnatal ages: newborn, 2-4 months, and 8-12 months.

Procedure

After reviewing the newborn and maternal medical records and determination of fulfillment of selection criteria was made, the parent(s) was approached to obtain consent for their infant's participation in the study. After informing them of the purpose and general nature of the study, agreeable parent(s) filled out an informed consent form (see Appendix C). Then the infants were transported from either the mother's room or the newborn nursery to the newborn laboratory. This generally occurred within an hour after their last feeding. They were placed in the basinette in a supine position and then recording sensors were attached.

Procedures were similar for older infants. Upon arrival at the psychology laboratory, the parent(s) were informed of the purpose and general nature of the study and then they filled out an informed consent form (see Appendix C). Functions of the sensors were explained during their application and any questions were answered. The parent then brought the infant into the testing room where they usually proceeded to feed the infant. After feeding, the infant was placed upon the mattress in the testing chamber and the parent or an experimenter stayed with the infant until it fell asleep. It should be noted that a subset of infants 2-4 months (n=12) were tested while laying supine in an infant seat such that they were elevated about 45 degrees; whereas the rest of these older infants 2-4 months (n=11) and the 8-12 month infants were tested while lying flat in the supine position.[2] Once their infant was asleep, the parent returned to the main laboratory room and answered a set of health questions relating to the obstetrical history, delivery of the infant and neonatal course (see Appendix A).

Testing began once the infant was asleep and the physiological signals were checked for clarity and appropriate gain, and continued as long as the subject remained asleep. See Table 1, 2, and 3 for a listing of the stimulus sequence (SEQ) assigned to each infant. Stimulus presentation required the experimenter to hold the tip of the air tube at about 8 cm from the stimulus site and maintain that position for the duration of the ten-second stimulus. Airstream presentations to the face were

directed toward the dorsum of the nose and accordingly
also stimulated the forehead and eyelids. Airstream
presentations to the abdomen were directed just rostral
to the umbilicus. The intertrial interval varied randomly
between 40 and 60 seconds. After each trial the
experimenter recorded status of state-relevant behaviors
occurring during the ten seconds prior to and following
stimulus onset. Behaviors assessed were the infant's
eyelid position, presence or absence of rapid eye movements
(REM), presence or absence of small or large movement
(i.e., small movement consisted of fine motor movement,
sucking bursts, and grimaces; large movement consisted of
gross limb or torso movement, for example, startle or
struggling), presence or absence of soft or loud
vocalizations and wakefulness (see Appendix B). The
testing-chamber air temperature recorded during testing
averaged 24.7±1 degrees centigrade.

Data Quantification

The state-relevant behavioral ratings were evaluated
in a post hoc manner for each trial based on Prechtl's
(1974) criteria. Only trials when infants were in active
sleep (AS), quiet sleep (QS) or transition (TS) between AS
and QS were included in the analysis. A six-point scale
was devised to rate the sleep state prior to trial onset.
Two points were allotted for observation of rapid eye

movement (REM); one point each was given for observation of soft vocalizations and small movements. If large movement occurred before trial onset then the trial was eliminated from the analysis. Respiration was scored from the physiograph recordings into three categories based upon the variability of the inspiratory amplitude and the interinspiratory interval; these categories were uniform-regular respiration (scored as 0), moderately irregular respiration (scored as 1) and very irregular respiration (scored as 2). A total score from behavioral and respiratory sources (ranging from 0 to 6) of two or less was considered QS; whereas a score of four or greater was labelled AS and a score of three points was judged to be TS. It was further stipulated that a total score of two, which was composed entirely of either REM or very irregular respiration would be rated as TS if it occurred within three trials (which is about three minutes) of a previously rated AS trial. As a further check on the state ratings, respiratory variability in six subjects was calculated according to the following formula, which has been quantitatively related to sleep states (Ver Hoeve & Leavitt, 1983); the trial median value of the $SD(i-i)/mean(i-i)$, where i-i is the interinspiratory interval, is greater than .2 for AS and less than .2 for QS. The values obtained for these six subjects confirmed the relationship between Ver Hoeve and Leavitt's respiratory variability quotient and sleep state as determined by the six-point behavioral rating scale.

Apnea frequency, latency from stimulus onset and duration were scored from the polygraph records. Apnea in response to the airstream stimulus was defined as a cessation of breathing for any duration greater than the pre-trial onset mean interinspiratory interval with a latency no greater than 20 seconds. Apnea was usually accompanied by a preceding breath. Apnea latency was scored as the amount of elapsed time from stimulus onset to apnea onset. The duration of apnea was determined by measuring the amount of elapsed time from apnea onset to the onset of the first inspiration terminating the apnea.

To measure HR each R-wave of the EKG was converted on-line by a peak detector to a square wave pulse which the PDP 8/E psychology computer used to measure the interbeat intervals to the nearest msec for two seconds before and 25 seconds after trial onset. This process was performed off-line for the newborn HR data by replaying the recorded pulses derived from each R-wave through the peak detector and PDP 8/E computer. These data were converted into HR in beats per minute (bpm) for each one second period in accordance with Graham's (1978) recommendations. The mean

HR response was computed for each subject for both within-subject conditions collapsing across trials. Since apnea could have any latency up to 20 seconds, it's effect on the HR response from stimulus onset would include this variability. Therefore, to determine the effect of apnea on HR, the HR response was scored from apnea onset as well as from stimulus onset. For the apnea-onset data set HR was scored second-by-second for the six seconds preceding and for the 25 seconds after apnea onset.

Notes

1. Because the procedures for acquiring subjects differed for NBs and older infants there were some differences in sample characteristics. There were more black infants in the newborn group than in the two groups of older infants. Also, compared to the NBs, the older infant groups, respectively, displayed significantly heavier birth weights, $t(22)=3.3$, $p<.01$ and $t(14)=2.5$, $p<.05$, were born to significantly older mothers, $t(22)=3.6$, $p<.001$ and $t(14)=2.4$, $p<.05$, and had reliably greater five minute APGAR scores, $t(22)=2.2$, $p<.05$ and $t(14)=3.0$, $p<.01$. There were no significant differences to emerge between the groups in gestational age at birth or in one minute APGAR scores. To assess the effects of race, birth weight, maternal age, APGAR score on the cardiorespiratory responses would reduce the sample size to the extent that comparisons could not be performed. As a result some of the findings may be accounted for by these differences.

2. The effect of elevating the 2-4 month-old infants 45 degrees as opposed to allowing them to lay flat in the supine posture was examined for each of the respiration response measures. Neither the main effect of posture nor any interaction with posture emerged significant. Therefore, these subjects were collapsed into one group for all analyses.

CHAPTER 3
RESULTS

The factors of critical interest in this study were the site of airstream stimulation and the age of the infant when tested. Knowledge of these effects indicate whether cardiorespiratory responses to stimulation of the facial region supplied by the ophthalmic branch of the trigeminal nerve may be unique and if so, whether it changes throughout the first year of life. However, the behavioral observations revealed that two other factors, sleep state and presence of elicited-large movement, may also have influenced the cardiorespiratory response. Before the effects of these two latter factors on the cardio-respiratory response could be examined, it was necessary to assess the infants' sleep state pattern during testing and to determine the extent to which large movement was elicited by the airstream stimuli.

Sleep State Incidence and Pattern

Table 4 presents the percentage of trials in which the sleep state of the infants were rated as QS, TS and AS across the age groups. The most notable finding was that the majority of data were collected while the infants were in QS. However, the NB group tended to exhibit a

53

TABLE 4

Percent of Trials in Quiet Sleep (QS), Active Sleep (AS)
and Transitional Sleep (TS) States

Age

State	NB	2-4	8-12	Mean
QS	74.97	89.63	93.60	86.07
AS	17.17	4.39	3.35	8.30
TS	7.86	5.99	3.05	5.63

little less QS and a little more AS than the two older
groups. Despite this age difference, a clear cycling of
sleep states over the course of the testing session
emerged. Figure 1 depicts the mean sleep state ratings of
the three age groups over the twenty-trial session. It
appeared that, although the infants mean state ratings were
closer to QS throughout the session, more infants were
rated in AS or TS at the beginning of the session. As
testing proceeded, the state of the infants shifted toward
QS and by the end of the session state appeared to shift
back toward TS. The confirming analyses can be found in
Appendix D. Because sleep state did vary with age and
across the session, its possible effects were assessed or
controlled whenever feasible in the cardiorespiratory
analyses.[1]

Large Movement Incidence

Behavioral observations of the ten seconds post-trial
onset indicated that infants in each age group occasionally
produced large movements (LM) in response to the airstream
stimulus. In these cases the reaction often had a
superficial resemblence to a startle or Moro reflex and
included abduction of the shoulders, extension of the legs,
arms, elbows, wrists and fingers and on occasions an
arching of the back. In other cases of LM, brief

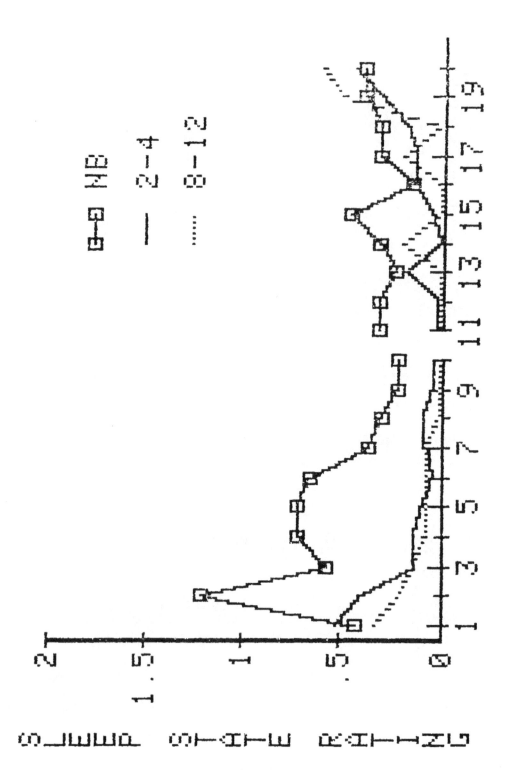

TRIALS

Figure 1. Mean Sleep State Rating for the First and Last Ten Trials.
Newborn (NB), 2-4 and 8-12 month infants are contrasted; a rating of two
was active sleep, one was transitional sleep and zero was quiet sleep.

struggling movements were observed including movements of arms, torso and head. Also, a combination startle and then struggle was sometimes observed. If the LM lasted more than 15 seconds then the trial was eliminated from analysis.

Table 5 presents the mean percent of face and abdomen trials in which LM was elicited by the airstream stimulus for all age groups. Analyses of these data (see Appendix E) revealed that the percent of elicited LM was not significantly affected by the sleep state of the infant, although there were age differences observed.[1] In NB infants, the airpuff elicited substantially more LM than was elicited in the older groups, being reduced from nearly half of all trials at birth to well under ten percent by one year. Furthermore, only the NB group displayed more LM to the facial than to the abdominal airpuff. The other two groups showed no such differential sensitivity to the stimulus.

There is no question that the presence of a LM will exert a powerful effect on the cardiac and respiratory activity. Its effects changed with age and site of stimulation and, like the effects of sleep state, were assessed or controlled in the cardiorespiratory analyses to follow.

TABLE 5

Percent of Trials with Large Movement Elicited by
Face (F) and Abdomen (A) Airstream Stimulation

Age

Condition	NB	2-4	8-12	Mean
F	54.50	13.99	3.44	23.98
A	35.72	9.26	7.33	17.45
Mean	45.11	11.63	5.39	

Respiration Response to Airstream Stimulation

The airstream stimulus resulted in the production of
apnea in most infants. In this section of the results the
effects of the independent variables were determined
respectively for the percent of apnea elicited, latency to
apnea onset and duration of apnea. However, it wasn't
possible to include all four variables in an overall
analysis simultaneously, since this would leave many
unfilled cells. However, the a priori variables of age and
site of stimulation were included in all analyses.
Initially, age and site were evaluated ignoring both state
and movement variation. In subsequent analyses the effects
of sleep state and LM were added to age and site
variables. Since the preliminary analyses indicated that
sleep state had an effect only on the percent of apnea
elicited and not on apnea latency and duration, the results
in the latter two response measures were simplified by
collapsing across the state variable.

Percent of Elicited Apnea

Effect of airstream stimulation site. Table 6 lists
the mean percent of trials in which apnea was elicitied by
facial and abdominal airstream stimuli across all age
groups for the data collapsed across state and also
for the QS state alone data. In general, the facial

TABLE 6

Percent of Trials with Apnea Elicited by Airstream Stimulation
of the Face (F) and Abdomen (A) When Sleep State Is
Ignored (All States) and When Infants Were in Quiet Sleep (QS)

Age

State	Condition	NB	2-4	8-12	Mean
All States	F	30.15	25.46	8.86	21.93
	A	11.66	5.40	1.94	6.09
QS alone	F	22.03	22.44	8.76	18.38
	A	6.45	4.96	1.67	4.41
Mean		17.57	14.57	5.30	

airpuff elicited apnea on a greater percentage of trials than the abdominal airpuff. Also, age was a powerful factor with a three-fold decrement over age in the percent of elicited apnea occurring predominantly between the older two groups.

The statistical reliability of these effects were initially assessed using all of the data (i.e., ignoring sleep state). The results of this analysis revealed significant main effects of Age, $F(2/49)=6.6$, $p<.005$, and Sites, $F(1/49)=3.7$, $p\leq.001$. This confirms both the decrease in the percent over age and the greater effect of the facial airpuff seen in the Table 6 means. When the analysis was restricted to just the younger groups, only a Sites effect, $F(1/35)=33.0$, $p<.001$, emerged. The lack of significant Age effect indicated that, even though the facial airpuff exceeded the abdominal airpuff, the percent of apnea elicited by either stimulus site did not differ between the younger two age groups. However, when the two older groups were contrasted, a significant interaction between Age and Sites, $F(1/36)=4.7$, $p<.05$, emerged. Subanalysis revealed that this interaction arose because there was greater frequency of apnea elicited by the facial airpuff in the 2-4 infants than the 8-12 infants, $F(1/36)=6.4$, $p<.05$; whereas, no significant difference emerged in the percent of apnea elicited by the abdominal airpuff. Thus facial airstream stimulation induced apnea on a greater percent of trials in the younger groups and markedly less in the 8-12 group.

Effect of sleep state. Analysis of the percent of apnea elicited when infants were in QS revealed that the same effects of age and stimulation site were found. However, inspection of Table 6 suggests that restricting the data to QS reduced the frequency of apnea, especially for the NBs. Therefore, the QS only data were compared to the data which included AS and TS as well as QS trials.[1] This resulted in a significant interaction between State and Age, $F(2/49)=7.2$, $p<.005$. This interaction was not maintained when the two older groups were analysed, indicating no effect of state for these infants. However, when the NB group was analysed, a significant State effect emerged, $F(1/13)=10.5$, $p<.01$, indicating that when NB infants were in QS a significant reduction in the percent of apnea was elicited by both facial and abdominal stimuli The face still elicited greater percent of apnea than did abdominal airstream stimulation, $F(1/13)=10.4$, $p<.01$.

Effect of preceding large movement. The following analyses were performed to determine whether the percent of elicited apnea would be influenced by the presence or absence of LM occurring after trial onset but prior to apnea onset.[2] Table 7 presents the mean percent of elicited

TABLE 7
Percent of Trials with Apnea Elicited by Airstream
Stimulation of the Face (F) and Abdomen (A) When Preceded by
Large Movement (LM) and When Large Movement Was Absent (No LM)

Age

Condition	Movement	NB	2-4	8-12	Mean
F	LM	30.07	57.31	40.00	42.69
	No LM	22.45	18.96	2.86	17.97
	Mean	26.26	38.14	21.43	
	N	14	13	5	
A	LM	26.09	13.33	14.29	18.48
	No LM	7.87	3.84	1.43	4.94
	Mean	16.98	8.59	7.86	
	N	14	15	7	

apnea as a function of trials with LM and trials with no LM
for each stimulus site and age group. As is evident from
the table, apnea was much more common following LM than
when LM was absent. This was true for both face and
abdomen trials, but overall, the facial airpuff still
elicited apnea on a greater percent of trials than did the
abdominal airpuff. A more surprising finding, however, was
that the effect of preceding LM was to reverse the pattern
of face-elicited apnea across age. That is, apnea
following LM was least common in NBs and most common in the
older groups. This reversal of the pattern of apnea
frequency when apnea was preceded by LM is difficult to
interpret in view of the small percent of trials with LM
elicited (see Table 5). Conversely, without LM the pattern
of face-elicited apnea over age remained as reported
above, with most apnea elicited in the two younger groups
and much less apnea elicited in the 8-12 infants.

The data were initially analysed with an ANOVA
contrasting the effects of presence or absence of LM as
well as stimulation Site across Age. Both LM and non-LM
data, respectively, yielded significant effects of Site,
$F(1/23)=9.7$, $p<.01$ and $F(1/48)=15.1$, $p<.001$, indicating
that whether or not LM preceded apnea, the facial airpuff
elicited greater percent of apnea than did the abdominal
airpuff. Analyses of each stimulus site were performed

separately to contrast the effects of LM on the frequency
of apnea elicited. Significant LM effects of, $F(1/29)=13.5$,
$p<.005$ and $F(1/33)=5.2$, $p<.05$, for face and abdomen sites
respectively were found. Inspection of Table 7 indicated
that these LM effects were the result of greater percent of
apnea preceded by LM than by no LM. Although the
interaction between Age and LM failed to reach significance
for the analysis of abdominal trials, this interaction came
close to reaching significance, $F(2/29)=2.5$, $p<.10$, for the
analysis of face trials. This provided suggestive, albeit
weak, evidence that the pattern of face-elicited apnea may
differ between age groups depending on whether or not LM
preceded apnea.

Exploratory analyses confirmed this suspicion by a
separate analysis of the LM and non-LM data, which
contrasted the percent of apnea elicited by the face
stimulus. Differing age trends appeared depending upon
whether or not LM preceded apnea. When it preceded apnea,
NB infants exhibited a lower percent of apnea than the 2-4
infants, $F(1/20)=4.1$, $p<.05$. There were no significant
differences between the older groups. When no LM preceded
apnea, no significant differences were found between the
two younger groups. A significant decrease, however, in
the percent of apnea between the 2-4 and 8-12 infants,
$F(1/35)=4.5$, $p<.05$, emerged. Therefore, apnea elicited by

the facial airpuff, if preceded by LM, increased with age from NB to 2-4 and 8-12 months. Conversely, apneic episodes unaffected by LM resulted in no difference between the NB and 2-4 groups; whereas, the 8-12 infants displayed a marked reduction in the percent of apnea elicited by the facial airpuff.

Latency to Apnea Onset

Effect of airstream stimulation site. Table 8 depicts the mean latency in seconds from trial onset to apnea onset for face and abdomen trials across all age groups. The latency to apnea onset was initially analysed with an ANOVA contrasting the effects of Site of stimulation across Age. This analysis yielded an interaction between Age and Sites, $F(2/17)=2.6$, which was not quite significant at the $p<.11$ level. No significant difference was found between the two older groups when they were compared. However, the NBs' latency to apnea onset elicited by the facial airpuff were significantly shorter than the apnea latencies elicited by the abdominal airpuff, $F(1/9)=4.8$, $p<.05$. Therefore, the site of airstream stimulation had no effect on the two older groups. However, the facial airpuff did act to induce apnea sooner than the abdominal airpuff in the NB infants.

Effect of preceding large movement. The next analysis was undertaken to determine if the apnea latency differed on trials in which LM preceded apnea as compared to trials

TABLE 8

Latency to Apnea Onset in Seconds as Elicited by Airstream
Stimlulation of the Face (F) and Abdomen (A)

Age

Condition	NB	2-4	8-12	Mean
F	4.27	7.09	13.10	6.28
A	8.20	8.97	7.25	8.41
Mean	6.23	8.03	10.18	
N	10	8	2	

in which LM was absent. Since there were too few cells in
which apnea was elicited by the abdomen airpuff, analyses
were performed across age groups only for trials with apnea
elicited by the facial airpuff, which was the main
condition of interest. In Table 9 little effect of LM can
be seen on the latency to apnea. Separate analyses[3] of both
LM and non-LM trials respectively revealed shorter apnea
latencies in NBs than the 2-4 infants, of $F(1/19)=5.9$ and
$F(1/13)=6.7$, both at $p<.05$. No significant difference was
found between the two older groups. Therefore, latency to
apnea onset was shorter in the NBs than the older infants
regardless of whether LM preceded apnea or not. Although
LM seemed to delay apnea onset by about two seconds, this
observation could not be assessed by statistical comparison
of LM and non-LM data[3].

Duration of Apnea

Effect of airstream stimulation site. Inspection of
Table 10 revealed that the facial airpuff induced apnea of
greater duration than the airpuff to the abdomen. As well,
the NBs apnea was about half as long as the apnea induced
in the older groups. The initial ANOVA of the duration of
apnea yielded significant main effects of Site,
$F(1/17)=8.9$, $p<.05$, and Age, $F(2/17)=8.9$, $p<.005$,
indicating that the facial airpuff elicited more prolonged

TABLE 9
Latency to Apnea in Seconds Elicited by Airstream
Stimulation of the Face When There Was Preceding
Large Movement (LM) and When Large Movement Was Absent (No LM)

Age

Movement	NB	2-4	8-12	Mean
LM	6.00	9.73	9.80	7.96
N	10	8	2	
No LM	2.55	5.81	7.41	5.28
N	8	13	7	

TABLE 10
Duration of Apnea in Seconds Elicited by Airstream
Stimulation of the Face (F) and Abdomen (A)

Age

Condition	NB	2-4	8-12	Mean
F	4.86	8.41	11.53	6.94
A	3.41	6.26	10.60	5.25
Mean	4.14	7.30	11.06	
N	10	8	2	

apnea than the abdominal airpuff across all age groups.
Subanalysis revealed that the Age effect arose from less
prolonged apnea in the NB group than the 2-4 group,
$F(1/16)=7.6$, $p<.05$, but no significant difference between
the older groups.

Effect of preceding large movement. Table 11 depicts
the mean apnea duration induced by the facial airpuff when
apnea followed LM and when no LM preceded apnea across age
groups. To assess this, LM and no LM data were analysed
separately.[3] In both analyses, as reported above, more
prolonged apnea was elicited in the older groups than the
NB infants. This was confirmed when an analysis of the two
younger groups yielded significant Age effects for trials
with LM, $F(1/19)=6.2$, $p<.05$, and for trials with no LM,
$F(1/19)=6.1$, $p<.05$. The analyses of the two older groups
revealed no significant Age effects for either LM or no LM
data. Although direct comparison between trials with LM
and trials with no LM could not be made, inspection of the
means in Table 11 indicated little effect of LM on the
duration of apnea. This, coupled with the fact that the
relationships between the age groups remained unaffected in
separate analyses of LM and no LM, provided tentative
support for the claim that the presence of preceding LM had
little or no effect on the duration of apnea.

TABLE 11
Duration of Apnea in Seconds Elicited by Airstream
Stimulation of the Face When There Was Preceding
Large Movement (LM) and When Large Movement Was Absent (No LM)

Age

Movement	NB	2-4	8-12	Mean
LM	4.46	9.53	7.00	6.89
N	10	13	7	
No LM	4.48	8.71	10.87	8.04
N	8	13	7	

Summary of the Respiration Response to Airstream Stimulation

These results provide clear evidence that both the
site receiving the airstream stimulation and the age of the
infant affected the frequency, latency and duration of
apnea. Facial stimulation appeared more effective
regardless of which measures were employed; it evoked apnea
more frequently than did abdominal stimulation, with longer
durations and shorter latencies. As well, in the absence
of LMs, the facial airstream produced apnea more frequently
in infants younger than four months than in older infants.
Large movements preceding apnea were generally associated
with more frequent apnea and perhaps also resulted in
somewhat longer latencies; these effects were more evident
in the older two groups of infants. However, the effects
of LM in these infants were of questionable significance,
since on most trials no LM was evoked. For NBs, apnea
occurred with shorter latency and duration than the older
infants. State effects seemed only to influence the
frequency at which apnea could be elicited in NBs, with
overall reduction during QS for both face and abdomen
trials; otherwise, QS state did not differentially affect
apnea frequency over age or stimulation site.

In sum, these results suggested a developmental trend
in the maturation of respiratory inhibition induced by
airstream stimulation of the face. The NBs, as a group

were very sensitive to stimulation of the face, which
induced frequent apneic episodes that were tempered by
their short duration. Conversely, the 8-12 month-old
infants produced less frequent but longer apnea. Most
notably, however, the 2-4 month-old infants, from the point
of view of vulnerability for SIDS, combined the worst
characteristics of both groups; in these infants apneas
were elicited with an elevated frequency equivalent to that
of the NBs but with a prolonged duration similar to that of
the older infants.

HR Response Topography

From the analysis of the respiration results it was
clear that the questions of most significance to the main
hypotheses were those pertaining to the role of facial
airstream stimulation in the induction of apnea,
uncomplicated by the effect of LM. Of secondary interest
was whether differential HR changes to the airstream
stimuli directed to the face and abdomen were evident when
no alteration in respiration occurred. Therefore, the
analyses of the HR response were performed on two subsets
of the data to determine whether the response topography
was affected differentially by a) the site of airstream
stimulation when no apnea was elicited; and b) the presence
or absence of apnea to facial stimulation.

Prestimulus Levels

Prior to the analysis of the HR response topography the prestimulus levels of HR were evaluated to determine whether the post-stimulus HR response could have been influenced by initial prestimulus levels. This was of particular concern since it was to be expected that prestimulus levels would co-vary with infant age (Harper et al., 1982). Table 12 depicts the mean HR values in beats per minute (bpm) for the second preceding stimulus onset across the age groups during trials with and without elicited-apnea.

The analysis of the prestimulus HR level in the trials in which no apnea or LM were elicited used Age as the between-subject factor and Site of stimulation as the within-subject factor. Only the Age effect was significant, $F(2/47)=5.9$, $p<.01$. With no significant difference between the two younger groups, the difference between the age groups, therefore, can be accounted for by diminished prestimulus levels in the 8-12 infants.[4]

Post-stimulus Changes

The interpretation of the post-stimulus HR response topography is complicated by the apparent relationship between prestimulus HR levels and the infants postnatal age. Hence, the post-stimulus HR levels and perhaps topography may be partially determined by the prestimulus

TABLE 12

Mean Prestimulus HR Levels in bpm in the Presence and Absence of
Apnea and Large Movement (LM) for Facial (F) and Abdominal (A)
Airstream Stimulation Trials

Age

Apnea	Movement	Condition	NB	2-4	8-12	Mean
No	No LM	F	117.92	122.76	110.52	117.83
		A	118.72	122.17	112.11	118.26
		Mean	118.32	122.47	111.32	
		N	13	22	15	
Yes	LM	F	123.56	130.03	106.65	124.90
		N	11	10	2	
Yes	No LM	F	121.21	121.45	117.16	120.31
		N	8	13	7	

HR levels. This statistical problem is known as the Law of Initial Values as outlined by Wilder (1950). Following the guidelines suggested by Richards (1980) for countering the effects of prestimulus HR on postimulus HR, the assumption of homogeneity of regression coefficients for the data were tested over age for regression of each of the 25 post-stimulus seconds on the first prestimulus second. Each of these analyses revealed that the assumption of homogeneity of regression coefficients was not violated. Therefore, the effects of the experimental parameters on the HR response topography could be compared across age. However, to control for the effects due to the Law of Initial Values, the analysis of covariance (ANACOVA) was used.[5]

Since the interpretation of HR change was of primary concern, difference scores were calculated by taking the algebraic difference between the prestimulus value and the post-stimulus values. The correlation between prestimulus and difference scores have typically been found lower than the correlation between prestimulus and post-stimulus scores (Benjamin, 1967). Therefore, the use of difference scores, herein, provided an additional statistical advantage. Despite lower correlations, however, difference scores still remain subject to the Law of Initial Values. The HR difference scores, therefore, were all analysed with ANACOVAs using the HR value in the second preceding stimulus

onset as the covariate, Age as the between-subject factor
and Seconds as the within-subject factor. It should be
noted that all significant effects reported below remained
significant when the conservative Greenhouse-Geisser
approximation of degrees of freedom was used (Greenhouse &
Geisser, 1959).

HR Response to the Airstream Stimulus: Face vs. abdomen

Figures 2 and 3 depict the HR change scores at each
age in response to facial and abdominal stimulation in the
absence of apnea and LM. For both stimulation sites these
figures show that the a short monophasic acceleration to
the airstream was produced by the NBs. However, the two
older groups displayed a triphasic response to the
airstream stimuli comprised of a brief deceleration
followed by an acceleration and a subsequent deceleration.
After stimulus offset HR levels in these infants gradually
recovered toward prestimulus levels.

More specifically, ANACOVA analyses (see Appendix F)
revealed that an initial deceleration was elicited in the
older infants within one second of stimulus onset but was
not elicited in the NBs. An acceleration followed
maximizing at the third post-stimulus second in all age
groups. This acceleration, which was greater when elicited
by the facial airpuff than by the abdominal airpuff,
differentiated all the age groups such that the 8-12

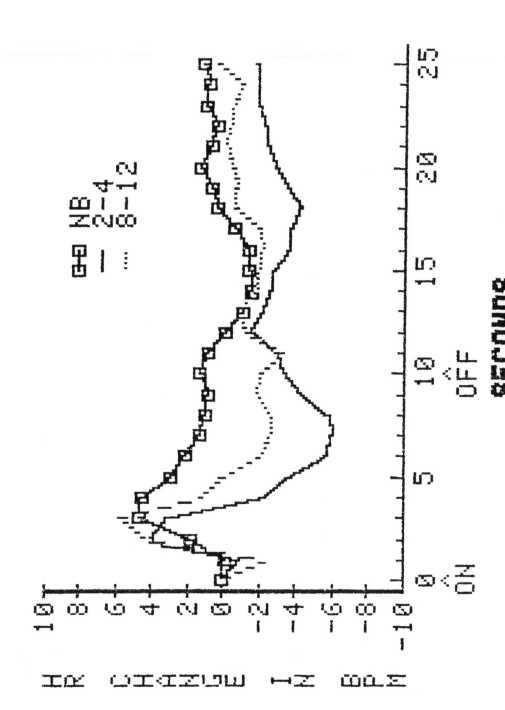

Figure 2. Mean HR Response to Facial Airstream Stimulation When No Apnea or Large Movement Were Elicited. The airpuff, as delivered to newborn (NB), 2-4 and 8-12 month infants, was initiated at second zero (ON) and terminated at second ten (OFF).

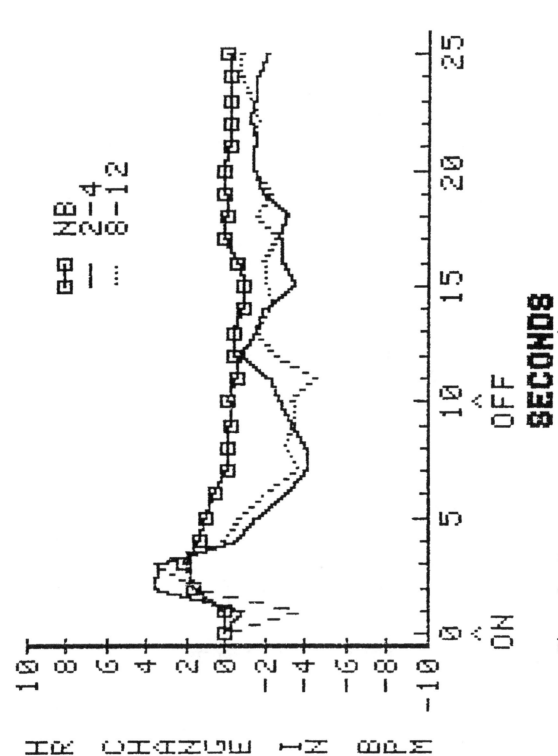

Figure 3. Mean HR Response to Abdominal Airstream Stimulation When No Apnea or Large Movement Were Elicited. The airpuff, as delivered to newborn (NB), 2-4 and 8-12 month infants, was initiated at second zero (ON) and terminated at second ten (OFF).

infants displayed the fastest acceleratory recruitment
followed by the 2-4 infants and then the NBs. As in the
early deceleration, the NBs were differentiated from the
older infants by the ensuing deceleration from seconds
three to ten, which reached its nadir by the seventh post-
stimulus second in the older infants but merely returned to
pretrial levels in the NBs. Only the 2-4 infants displayed
an effect of the stimulation site during this interval with
greater deceleration to the facial airpuff than the
abdominal airpuff. Following stimulus offset all groups
displayed a cubic trend over seconds 11 to 25, which was
unaffected by the stimulation site, appearing to decrease
slightly 5 to 10 seconds after stimulus offset followed by
a gradual return to pretrials levels.

HR Response to the Facial Airstream Stimulus: Apnea vs. no apnea

Figure 4 shows the response to facial stimulation when
apnea was present without preceding LM. By comparing these
responses with the responses in Figure 2 in which no apnea
was elicited by the facial airstream, the effect of apnea
elicitation on HR can be examined. Although the overall
topography of the response was similar with and without
apnea, when apnea was elicited, the older groups displayed
a more prolonged late deceleration which was of greater
magnitude than when no apnea was elicited. The NBs
response was unaffected by whether or not apnea was induced.

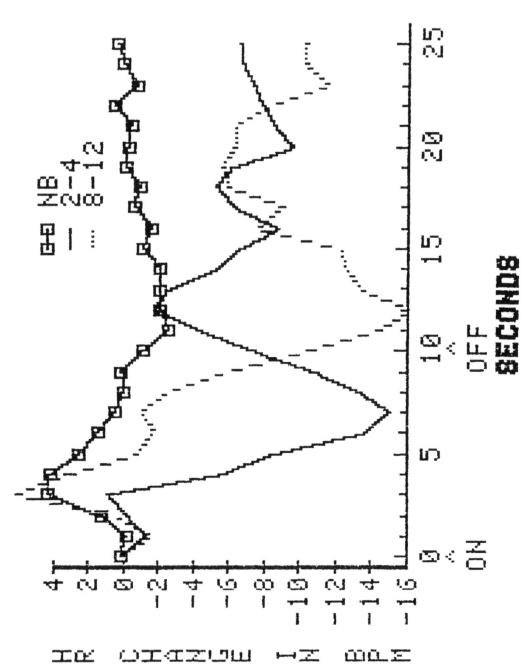

Figure 4. Mean HR Response to Facial Airstream Stimulation When Apnea Was
Elicited Without Preceding Large Movement. The airpuff, as delivered to newborn
(NB), 2-4 and 8-12 month infants, was initiated at second zero (ON) and
terminated at second ten (OFF).

The ANACOVAs of the overall HR response used seconds 1 to 25 as levels of the within-subject Seconds factor, Age as the between-subject factor and presence or absence of Apnea as the second within-subject factor.[6] A significant interaction between Age, Apnea and Seconds, $F(48/576)=2.0$, $p<.001$, was found. The next analysis examined whether the differences described by this interaction existed during the period of acceleration across seconds 1 to 3. It did not, since only a significant Seconds effect, $F(2/48)=6.7$, $p<.005$, emerged. Therefore, up to this point in the analysis the HR response was unaffected by the age of the infant or by the presence or absence of apnea.

The age groups were differentiated by the HR response during the late-deceleration from seconds 3 to 12, as indicated by a significant interaction between Age, Apnea and Seconds, $F(18/216)=3.1$, $p<.001$. The subanalysis consisted of examining the NB group alone. Only a significant linear trend across Seconds, $F(1/6)=21.1$, $p<.005$, was found, indicating that there was a linear HR decrement toward base level both in trials with apnea and trials without apnea. Subsequent t-tests revealed that the decrement in the NBs HR during this interval did not proceed below prestimulus levels. When the two older groups were contrasted a significant interaction between Age, Apnea and Seconds, $F(9/162)=4.7$, $p<.001$, emerged. This was due to changes in both magnitude and topography of the deceleration when apnea was elicited. When the two older groups were compared using only the non-apnea responses, only a significant quadratic trend over Seconds, $F(1/18)=7.5$, $p<.05$, emerged, indicating that there was no difference between groups in the magnitude of the deceleration when no apnea was elicited. However, on trials when apnea was elicited, the magnitude of deceleration was increased to a greater extent in the 8-12 infants than in the 2-4 infants, as substantiated by a significant interaction between Age and Seconds, $F(9/162)=6.3$, $p<.001$. Moreover, the effect of apnea was to prolong the deceleratory response differentially in these older infants. As can be seen in Figure 4, the deceleration in the 2-4 group reached its nadir and began its recovery toward pretrial levels sooner than the 8-12 infants. This was confirmed by an orthogonal trend analysis of each age group for apnea data only, with a significant decreasing quadratic trend over Seconds, $F(1/12)=31.6$, $p<.001$, for the 2-4 infants and a decreasing linear trend over Seconds, $F(1/6)=39.1$, $p<.001$, for the 8-12 infants.

The analysis of seconds 12 to 25, which represented the period of HR recovery, yielded a significant main effect of Apnea, $F(1/23)=7.0$, $p<.05$, and an interaction between Age

and a quadratic trend over Seconds, $F(2/24)=5.2$, $p<.05$.
Neither the effects of Apnea or Seconds nor their interaction
were significant when analysing only the NB group's HR
recovery, indicating that regardless of whether apnea or no
apnea was elicited the NB HR was stable throughout this
period maintaining a mean HR level of -0.65 bpm. When
comparing the younger groups only a significant Age effect,
$F(1/17)=6.2$, $p<.05$, was found, indicating that the 2-4
group operated at a lower level than the NB group, with
mean HR bpm levels of -0.65 and -5.01 for the NB and 2-4
groups respectively. When comparing the 2-4 and 8-12
groups, however, an interaction between Age, Apnea and
quadratic trend over Seconds, $F(1/18)=4.5$, $p<.05$, emerged.
No difference was found in the recovery trends of the
trials with no apnea. When apnea did occur, however, the
enhanced late-deceleration and the resultant phase
shift between these groups resulted in interacting
decreasing and increasing quadratic trends over Seconds,
$F(1/18)=7.5$, $p<.05$. Inspection of Figure 5 reveals that by
post-stimlulus second 12 the HR response of the 2-4 group
had partially recovered, while the 8-12 group had just
reached its nadir. Hence, HR levels decreased to a mean of
-7.25 bpm for the 2-4 infants while the HR levels increased
to a mean level of -8.58 bpm for the 8-12 infants.

In summary, the NBs HR response when apnea was elicited was not distinguishable from the response observed when no apnea was elicited.[7] The main effect of apnea on the HR response appeared in the older groups. Apnea resulted in an accentuated deceleration during seconds 3 to 12 post-stimulus onset reaching a maximum at seconds 7 and 12 respectively for the 2-4 and 8-12 groups. Apnea also had an effect on the HR recovery during seconds 12 to 25 in the older groups, exhibiting less tendency to return to pretrial levels.

HR Response to the Facial Airstream Stimulus from Apnea Onset

The previous HR analysis used HR values scored from stimulus onset. When apnea was present, it could occur anywhere in the trial within the 20-second post-stimulus observation window. Therefore, the topography of the HR response in the presence of apnea was difficult to interpret. This was especially the case, since the latency to apnea onset was significantly related to age, with older infants displaying longer apnea latencies. To obtain a more precise determination of the effect of apnea on the response topography, HR was aligned relative to apnea onset rather than stimulus onset. To maintain a constant standard of reference, these HR values, as in the above HR statistics, were represented relative to prestimulus level. For example, the HR value at second zero represented the HR difference from prestimulus level of the interval just preceding apnea onset.

The mean HR values observed during apnea as elicited by the facial airpuff (uncomplicated by LM) were plotted in Figure 5. The analysis of the HR response from apnea onset did not examine the effect of preceding LM on the HR topography. As can be seen in Figure 6, the effect of LM was to substantially increase HR (relative to prestimulus level) prior to apnea onset. Otherwise the response topography remained similar to the response when no LM preceded apnea. As can be seen in Figure 5, the HR response of the NBs was not affected by the production of apnea; whereas, in both of the older groups apnea induced rapidly-recruiting, large-magnitude decelerations, which began to recover to prestimulus levels when apnea terminated. Note that the arrowhead located below each curve in both Figures 5 and 6 corresponds to the point where apnea ended and breathing resumed.

ANACOVA of the no LM data (Figure 5) assessed the pre-apnea HR levels. Seconds -5 to 0 were used as levels of the Seconds factor, Age as the between-subject factor and the unadjusted HR value in the second preceding apnea onset (i.e., second 0) as the covariate. There were no differences to emerge during this period as neither the effects of Age or Seconds nor their interaction were significant.

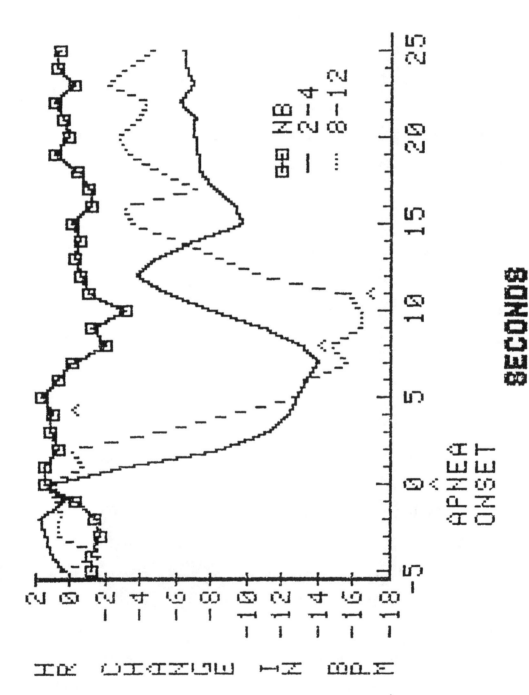

Figure 5. Mean HR Response to Facial Airstream Stimulation When Apnea Was Elicited Without Preceding Large Movement Adjusted from Apnea Onset. The arrowhead below each of the newborn (NB), 2-4 and 8-12 month infants' plots indicates the point of termination of apnea and resumption of breathing.

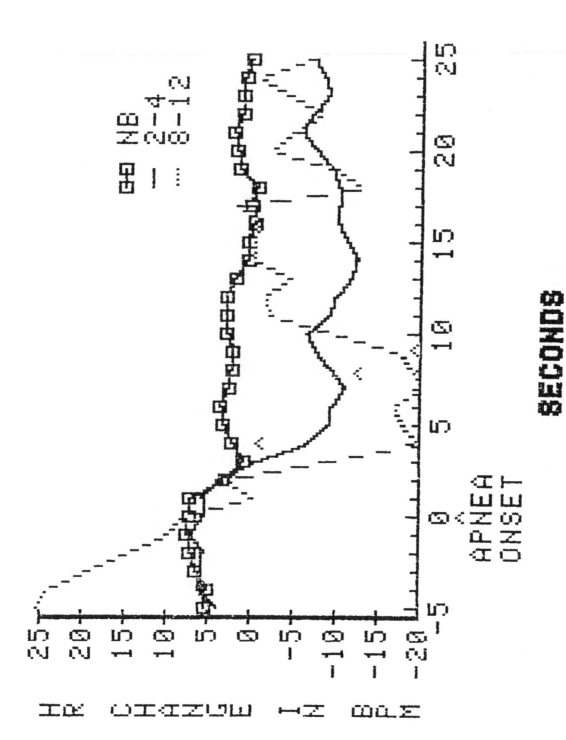

Figure 6. Mean HR Response to Facial Airstream Stimulation When Apnea Occurred Following Large Movement Adjusted from Apnea Onset. The arrowhead below each of the newborn (NB), 2-4 and 8-12 month infants' plots indicates the point of termination of apnea and resumption of breathing.

Inspection of the trends in Figure 5 suggested that there was an initial deceleration upon apnea onset in the older groups, which was absent in the NB infants. The analysis of this trend used seconds 0 to 9 as the period of deceleration after apnea onset. The ANACOVA yielded a significant Age effect, $F(2/24)=4.0$, $p<.05$, a Seconds effect, $F(9/225)=7.7$, $p<.001$ and a two-way interaction of these factors, $F(18/225)=1.9$, $p<.05$. The subanalysis of the most salient of these effects - the Age-by-Seconds interaction - consisted first of assessing whether there was a Seconds effect in the NB group alone; there was not, $F(9/63)=1.0$, indicating that when apnea was elicited it had no effect on the NBs HR response. An ANACOVA was then performed on the two older groups. Only a significant Seconds effect, $F(9/162)=4.6$, $p<.001$, was found. Therefore, from the onset of the apneic period to the ninth second of the trial, the two older groups exhibited HR deceleration, which was of similar magnitude and which was totally absent in the NB group. The 2-4 infants reached a maximum deceleration of -14.46 bpm at seven seconds post-apnea onset; whereas the 8-12 infants decelerated to -15.91 bpm by the ninth second after apnea began.

Analysis of seconds 9 to 25 was performed to assess the period of recovery from the apneic episode. The NB group displayed no significant change over these seconds, which was not surprising since apnea seemed to have no effect on HR previous to this point in time. When the two older groups were analysed, however, a significant interaction between Age and Seconds, $F(16/288)=5.4$, $p<.001$, emerged. An orthogonal trend analysis revealed an interaction of linear Seconds and Age, $F(1/18)=16.2$, $p<.001$, indicating that, indeed, the HR levels in both groups were recovering toward pretrial levels during this period but differed in the temporal aspects of the recovery.

In summary, when considering all the analyses of the HR response topography, the onset of the airstream stimulus to the face evoked a monophasic acceleration in NBs and a triphasic response in the two older groups. Only the older age groups displayed a brief initial deceleration and following the subsequent acceleration a deceleration occurred proceeding well below prestimulus levels. The NBs response was unaffected by apnea. Similarly, the acceleratory component of the older infants' responses were unaffected by apnea, but not so for the deceleratory component. This latter deceleration was two to three times larger on trials when apnea was present. Realignment of the responses on apnea trials to correspond to apnea onset revealed that the apnea produced an immediate monophasic deceleration very similar to the late deceleratory component in the stimulus aligned functions. The deceleration initiated by apnea onset did not differ between the two older groups and displayed a recruitment speed wherein approximately 80% of the deceleration occurred within 3-5 seconds after apnea onset.

Notes

1. The proportion of trials when infants were in AS or TS were too small to permit evaluation of the effects of sleep state. Therefore, the following strategy was adopted whereby response measures collected while subjects were in QS were compared to the entire data set collapsed across state to determine if the contribution of the non-QS (i.e., AS and TS) data were sufficient to cause a significant difference in the response being examined. A nonsignificant difference between these two data sets was interpreted as indicating that the inclusion of the AS and TS data were not sufficient to significantly alter the observed trends. Henceforth, the entire data set was used in further analyses, thereby improving the statistical power of the analyses by increasing the sample size that could be included. It was recognized that a nonsignificant difference between these data sets did not rule out the possibility that AS or TS may still have an unique effect on the data. It should be noted, however, that the predominance of QS in this data was a function of the fact that infants in AS tended to awaken when stimulated with the airstream. This coupled with the probable influence of background maturational differences in the organization of sleep states prevented a more in-depth investigation of the effect of AS and TS states on the response measures.

2. In this case we were assessing the percent of elicited apnea for those trials in which LM occurred compared to those trials where no LM occurred. This is quite different from asking the question, what percent of trials with apnea was preceded by LM. The latter question will yield an answer pertaining to the relative proportion of elicited apneic episodes that were preceded by LM as well as yielding the proportion of apneic episodes that were not preceded by LM. As it happens, of the 138 apneic episodes elicited in this study, LM preceded apnea onset on 67 (i.e., 48%) occasions and only twice did LM follow apnea offset. Therefore, 50% of all elicited apneic-episodes were not preceded or followed by any LM.

3. Few subjects contributed apnea data for both LM and no LM trials. Therefore, we were unable to perform a within-subjects analysis of the effect of LM or no LM on any of the apnea response measures. In some cases, indirect comparisons were possible wherein data from subjects who contributed LM were assessed separate from all subjects who contributed no LM results.

4. To parallel the post-stimulus analyses, the prestimulus levels of trials with apnea preceded by LM and no LM were also examined. As can be seen in Table 12, the means were in the same direction as the prestimulus levels exhibited on trials with no apnea elicited. Whereas, the Age effect for apnea trials with no preceding LM did not reach significance, it was significant for trials when apnea was preceded by LM, $F(2/20)=3.8$, $p<.05$.

5. The analysis of covariance (ANACOVA) removes the effects of the Law of Initial Values by a linear regression of the post-stimulus HR values on the prestimulus values. Specifically, it acts to reduce the sum of squares by covarying out the variance accounted for by the sum of the deviation crossproduct scores relative to the prestimulus HR. See Benjamin (1967) for a more in-depth treatment of the use of ANACOVA to counter the effects of the Law of Initial Values on HR data.

6. The analysis of the HR response from stimulus onset did not include an analysis of the data when LM preceded apnea, since the effect of LM was to result only in a large monophasic acceleraton preceding the secondary deceleration. Otherwise the topography of the HR response remained unaffected by LM preceding apnea.

7. It should be noted that a follow-up analysis was performed, since sleep state had an effect of the percent of apnea elicited in the NB subjects. The NB HR response when apnea was elicited during QS to the facial airpuff was compared to the HR response of the NBs when both QS and the effects of AS and TS were combined. No significant effects due to State nor its interaction with Seconds were found. This suggested that although the QS state tended to reduce the proportion of apnea, the HR response remained unaffected.

CHAPTER 4
DISCUSSION

The results of this study clearly demonstrate the effects of age and site of airstream stimulation on cardiorespiratory control. Facial cooling induced more frequent and prolonged apnea with shorter latency than abdominal stimulation in healthy, sleeping infants up to one year of age. There was no change in the frequency of apnea elicited by the abdominal airpuff over age. With facial airstream stimulation, the overall incidence of apnea was fairly level from newborn (NB) through 2-4 months of age but dropped precipitously by 8-12 months. This was particularly true in the absence of large movement (LM), wherein infants 8-12 months of age exhibited an 85% reduction in apnea incidence relative to the 2-4 month infants. However, in the presence of LM, the frequency of apnea increased with age such that infants older than two months displayed more frequent and prolonged apneic episodes than newborns. In each age group, LM was associated with a greater percent of facial trials with apnea than when no LM occurred. However, since LM was induced on only 14% or less of the trials in the older infants, in an absolute sense the apnea consequent to LM

94

represented only a small fraction of the total number of
apneic episodes elicited. In contrast, the NBs displayed
LM on about half of the trials, thereby elevating the
absolute incidence of apnea. This suggests that the
mechanisms which resulted in apnea following LM may play a
significant role in increasing apnea frequency in these
infants. When apnea was elicited by the facial airpuff,
the effect of preceding LM was to delay apnea onset
somewhat in all age groups. Regardless of whether or not
LM preceded apnea the duration was much longer in the older
infants than for the NBs.

When no apnea was elicited by the airstream stimulus
to the face or abdomen, a monophasic HR acceleration was
observed in the NBs; however, a triphasic deceleration-
acceleration-deceleration response was produced by the
older infants to airstream stimulation of either site. The
magnitude of the acceleratory component increased slightly
with age of the infant, although the peak was slightly more
prolonged in the NBs (see Figures 2 and 3). The facial
airpuff resulted in larger accelerations than the abdominal
airpuff in all age groups. The late-deceleration, unique
to the older infants, was somewhat greater for facial than
for the abdominal airpuff. The presence of apnea elicited
by the facial airpuff produced no change in the NBs cardiac
response. With the older infants, apnea resulted in a
substantially increased late-bradycardia compared to

the no apnea response and did not differ in magnitude between the 2-4 and 8-12 month infants. Moreover, this enhanced bradycardia, did not begin to recover until the apnea was terminated (see Figure 5).

In summary, the results demonstrated an increased propensity for facial cooling to evoke apnea differentially over age in healthy, sleeping infants. Evaluation of infant sleep state revealed that infants in this study were predominantly in quiet sleep. The non-quiet sleep data did not appear to have a substantial effect on the parameters examined, although due to the sparcity of this data its possible effects could not be evaluated. The infants of different ages were differentiated based on their cardiorespiratory responses to facial airstream stimulation. The NBs displayed frequent apnea to the facial airpuff but these were of short duration and had no effect upon their cardiac response. On the other hand, the facial airpuff elicited apnea infrequently in the 8-12 month infants, although when it occurred it was of longer duration and accompanied by bradycardia which was maintained for the duration of the apnea. From the point of view of vulnerability for SIDS, the 2-4 month infants displayed a tendency to produce what are presumably the most potentially deleterious combination of cardiorespiratory changes; apnea to the facial airpuff in these infants occurred with elevated incidence similar to that shown by the NBs but with prolonged duration and concomitant large-magnitude bradycardia similar to that shown by the 8-12 month infants. Therefore, exposure to facial cooling by airstream stimulation of the ophthalmic branch of the trigeminal nerve has revealed that the age between two to four months is the age of greatest susceptibility to respiratory inhibition and concomitant cardiac rate depression in the maturation of cardiorespiratory control in the first year of life.

Implication for Dive Reflex as the Mechanism
for Inducing Apnea and Bradycardia

This study was not designed to determine what central mechanisms were involved in the production of apnea in these infants but clearly by virtue of the enhanced incidence of apnea to facial airstream cooling in infants throughout the first year of life some significance must be attached to the region of the face that is supplied by the ophthalmic branch of the trigeminal nerve. The trigeminal nerve mediates pain and temperature sensation of the face and has been implicated in the mediation of afferent impulses responsible for the dive reflex (Anderson, 1963). Both the apnea and bradycardia of the dive reflex are present in decerebrate animals, implying that the central connections between the afferent and efferent limbs of the reflex are in the brainstem (Anderson, 1963). Therefore the increased propensity for cool facial stimulation to induce apnea in infants probably reflects the preeminant role in this study of these pathways of central neural sensory integration which may be similar to those which mediate the dive reflex in the adult.

The dive reflex has been presented as an adaptive mechanism for defense of the lungs where the reflex apnea and laryngeal closure that result serve to prevent inhalation of the water which evoked the response (Richardson & Peatfield, 1981). The concomitant cardiovascular changes involve a vagal-induced bradycardia and sympathetically-mediated constriction of systemic vessels. The circulatory effects of increased $PaCO_2$ and decreased PaO_2 further augment the bradycardia and peripheral vasoconstriction, which effectively acts to redistribute blood supply toward regions such as the brain, which are most vulnerable to oxygen deficit (Irving, Solandt, Solandt & Fisher, 1935). For a mechanism similar to the dive reflex to be operating, the following must be present and functional: 1) pathways of sensory transduction (i.e., temperature and/or tactile); 2) connections to central pathways that are capable of interrupting ongoing respiration; 3) connections to central pathways that are capable of overriding the action of the chemoreceptors on

central regions of inspiratory drive so as to maintain
inhibition; 4) mechanisms to allow inspiratory drive to be
disinhibited when stimulation ceases so that breathing can
be resumed; and 5) mechanisms of cardiovascular
compensation such as bradycardia and redistribution of
blood supply away from the periphery and toward the heart
and brain, which act to conserve oxygen and thereby permit
more prolonged apneic episodes. The present results
provide information relevant to each of these points and
each will be discussed in turn.

An examination of the infants' cardiorespiratory
responses to the facial airstream reflects a response of
increasing maturity and adaptability with age. When no
preceding LM occurred the facial airstream evoked frequent
apnea in the NBs and 2-4 month infants demonstrating the
integrity of the trigeminal nerve containing the afferent
limb of the reflex in these infants as well as the ability
of central mechanisms to inhibit respiration. The
mechanism of cessation of breathing to airpuff stimulation
in this study was central in origin and not due to
obstruction of the airways. This was the case because
evidence of obstruction would present itself during
recording as a cessation of nasal respiration but a
continuation of diaphragm movements. This did not occur in
any of the apneic episodes induced in any of the subjects

who were monitored with both measures of nasal airflow and diaphragm movement.

The much greater incidence of LM in the NBs than the older subjects to the airstream at either stimulation site probably reflects a greater reactivity in the NBs to the stimulus rather than indicating any differences in the maturity of sensory transduction. Active sleep was a state wherein the airstream stimulation was observed to be more likely than during QS to induce wakefulness in all infant groups. This suggests that the threshold for induction of the response may be altered in AS rendering the infants more susceptible to respiratory inhibition in QS. Arousal from sleep during a stimulus presentation was usually associated with struggling and vigorous directed movements away from the airstream. Thus arousal from sleep may be one possible mechanism of preventing or terminating a reflex apnea. The fact that the NBs were in AS more than the older infants may also have contributed to their increased motor reactivity to the airstream.

The shorter latency to apnea onset in the NBs reflects the greater ease with which breathing can be interrupted during sleep in these infants. More facial cooling was required to elicit apnea in the older infants as reflected by their longer response latencies. Therefore, the threshold for facial cooling to result in apnea may be higher in these older infants. If this was the case then the markedly reduced incidence of apnea in the 8-12 month infants relative to the 2-4 month infants indicates that the mechanisms driving respiration during sleep in the oldest infants were more resistant to interruption and probably more mature. However, when the reflex apnea was induced in the 8-12 month infants the latency to onset was about the same as the 2-4 month infants and the response appeared to be of similar magnitude. If the dive reflex is actually an adaptive response to protect the lungs from potential irritants then the infant is clearly subject to competing interests since the cessation of breathing in the extreme is also maladaptive. Therefore, it is reasonable to expect that, as the infant matures and is more capable of compensating for changes in the composition of inspired air, the threshold for facial cooling to induce a cessation of breathing would be elevated.

The NBs demonstrated brief durations of apnea, which were likely to cease prior to the offset of the facial airstream stimulus; whereas, the older infants displayed more prolonged apneic episodes which typically began prior to and terminated after stimulus offset. The inability of the stimulus to maintain the induced-apnea for its entire duration in the NBs suggests that the central mechanisms which mediated the reflex apnea were not able to sustain

the inhibition on respiratory drive. It could indicate
that the arterial and medullary chemoreceptor mechanisms in
the NB have a more substantial influence than those
inducing the apnea at this age. However, the maintenance
of apnea in the older infants for the remaining seconds of
the airpuff suggests more powerful central inhibition of
respiratory drive in these infants. There are several
possible explanations for this finding. One explanation
may be that the increasing duration of apnea with age could
reflect the increasing functional residual capacity with
maturity so that older infants due to their better
buffering systems can tolerate greater hypoxic and
hypercapnic changes. The persistance of apnea after
stimulus offset in the older subjects differs from findings
in adults where the apnea and bradycardia of the dive
reflex is time-locked to the eliciting stimulus (Hurwitz &
Furedy, 1979). However, the dive reflex has only been
recorded in adults while they were awake. Therefore, aside
from the disparity in age and the implied difference in
central neural cardiorespiratory maturation, the
persistence of apnea beyond stimulus offset in infants
could reflect the relative difficulty of reinitiating
breathing during sleep once breathing has been interrupted.

McCubbin and colleagues (1977) reported heart rate
decelerations to facial airstream stimuli occurred
irrespective of whether apnea occurred or not. On the

other hand, a clear distinction was observed in this study between the cardiac response when no apnea was elicited compared with the large-magnitude changes coincident with elicited-apnea. In the older infants the facial airstream elicited large-magnitude bradycardic responses with rapid onset, which were maintained for the duration of the concomitant apneic episode. These response-topography features of rapid recruitment, large magnitude and sustained response until breathing is resumed were characteristic of the adult bradycardic response to simulated dives of apneic-face immersion in water (Hurwitz & Furedy, 1979). Since peripheral blood flow and oxygen consumption were not measured in this study there was no way to determine whether the infants' cardiovascular changes during apnea resembled those oxygen-conserving adjustments associated with the dive reflex (i.e., cardiac output reduction and redistribution of blood flow toward those regions which cannot sustain anaerobic metabolism for prolonged durations). Nevertheless, the bradycardia in these infants probably utilized similar vagal efferent pathways. The NBs lack of alteration in cardiac rate during apnea suggests that the mechanisms governing cardiac rate change at this age may not be physiologically coupled with brief phasic changes in respiration, although there is evidence to indicate that this is not so for tonic

respiratory activity in newborns (Porges, 1979). Regardless
of whether or not the bradycardic response does represent a
component of an adaptive compensatory response to an
elicited-apnea, it is evident that by two months of
postnatal age the cardiac response is clearly coupled with
the apneic episode.

Topography of HR Response in the Absence of Apnea

When no apnea was elicited by the facial or abdominal
airstream stimuli the NBs produced a monophasic
acceleratory response maximizing at the third post-stimulus
second; whereas the older infants displayed a triphasic
response composed of an initial brief deceleration at post-
stimulus second one followed by an acceleration maximizing
at second three and then a larger-magnitude deceleration
which reached a minimum at about seventh post-stimulus
second. Lipton et al. (1966) using a five-second airstream
stimulus directed to the abdomen also reported a monophasic
acceleration in NBs maximizing between the third and fourth
post-stimulus second. The magnitude of acceleration
observed was much greater than displayed by the NBs in this
study but this was probably because the airstream intensity
was 2.5 times greater than that used in the present study.
Despite the elevated intensity of the airpuff employed by
Lipton et al. (1966), it was apparent from the figures
presented that the older infants 2.5 and 5 months of age

also displayed a triphasic HR change with a similar topography as that observed in this study. It should be noted that these infants displayed a much larger acceleratory magnitude than exhibited by the 2-4 month or 8-12 month infants in this study. Unfortunately, they did not plot enough post-stimulus data to determine if there were any effects of stimulus intensity on the magnitude of the late-deceleration. Thus the difference in stimulus intensity employed by Lipton et al. (1966) and that used in the present study may account for the relative difference in acceleratory response magnitude to the abdominal airstream.

The slightly larger acceleration to the facial airstream than to the abdominal airstream in this study suggests that for a given airstream intensity airstream stimulation of the face will result in somewhat greater cardiac rate change. This suggests that there may be regional differences in the thermal sensitivity to airstream stimulation. It has been observed that the face displays greater sensitivity for warm thermal stimuli than the rest of the body (Stevens, Marks & Simonson, 1974). Although the appropriate studies have not yet been performed it is likely that facial preeminance is also the case for cold thermal sensitivity, since the number of cold receptors in the face are considerably greater per unit of surface area than in any other region of the body (Guyton, 1981). Hence it is reasonable to suggest that the face was probably more sensitive to the cooling aspects of the airstream stimulation than was the abdomen.

Regardless of whether the face was more thermally sensitive than the abdomen, differences in the magnitude of the cardiac rate changes in the absence of LM and apnea were only slight and the overall ontogeny of the HR response topography over age was the same to either stimulus. That is, for both stimuli a similar shift in HR topography emerged whereby the neonates displayed a monophasic HR acceleration and the older infants exhibited the triphasic response. Lipton et al. (1966) suggested that this shift in HR topography over age, which they also observed, probably reflected maturation of the autonomic nervous system; in particular, it was posited that the presence of early and late decelerations in only the older infants and the observation of increasing magnitude of deceleration of the early component with age was due to increasing vagal control over cardiac function. However, neonates are capable of producing deceleratory responses to stimuli in a variety of sensory modalities (e.g., Adkinson & Berg, 1976; Porges, Stamps & Walter, 1974; Pomerleau-Malcuit & Clifton, 1971; Sameroff, Cashmore & Dykes, 1973). Hence, based solely on the evidence of the lack of

deceleratory components, it is difficult to conclude that
vagal control was not sufficiently developed in the NBs.

Berg and Berg (1979) reviewed evidence which suggested
that the di- or tri-phasic HR response represented a
unique cardiac response which differed from the monophasic
long-duration deceleration of the orienting response in
the sensitivity or lack thereof to aspects of the steady-
state portions of the stimulus. Others have reinterpreted
the data to suggest that the direction of the HR change in
neonates was dependent on the intensity and complexity of
the stimulus such that low-intensity, simple stimuli with
controlled slow-rise times resulted in HR deceleration
while highly-intense, complex stimuli with uncontrolled
rise times produced HR acceleration (Graham, Anthony &
Zeigler, in press); these authors maintained that the
diphasic response[1] was not dependent on either high
intensity or sustained stimulus features. They cite
supporting evidence of a diphasic response evoked by a
range of stimuli intensities from 45 to 105 dB SPL, with
the acceleratory component increasing with increasing
intensity in neonates and one to ten month infants who were
asleep. Other evidence suggests that state may be
particularly relevant in the production of this response.
Pomerleau-Malcuit and Clifton (1973) provided evidence of
the effect of state on the HR response to a ten-second

tactile stimulus to the forehead of neonates. They
observed HR deceleration in awake infants before feeding
but this same stimulus induced a monophasic acceleration
while asleep. Berg, Berg and Graham (1971) documented this
HR pattern shift with state change in four-month old
infants to auditory stimulation. They observed that in
response to 50 and 75 dB tones with controlled fast and
slow rise times awake infants produced large monophasic
decelerations but as their state changed from alertness to
drowsiness and then to sleep the HR topography changed to a
triphasic response. Rewey (1973) also observed this same
shift from monophasic deceleration when awake to a
triphasic change when sleepy in response to short and long
75 dB continuous and pulsed tones in three month-old
infants; whereas the six week-old infants' response was
more variable and appeared to shift from a small
deceleration when awake to a diphasic response when
asleep. Adults also display a triphasic HR response to a
broad range of intensity of acoustic stimulation when
asleep (Berg, Jackson & Graham, 1975). It was reported
that as the intensity of the stimulus progressed from 30 to
75 dB the magnitude of each of the components of the
triphasic HR response increased. In sum, it appears that
the shift from a monophasic HR acceleration in NBs to a
triphasic HR response occurs in infancy between six weeks

and two months of age and is maintained into adulthood.
This response topography is affected by state such that the
triphasic response will not occur if the infant is awake.
Stimulus intensity appears to alter the magnitude of the
components of the response but otherwise the overall
response topography remains unaffected. Therefore, the
shift in HR topography observed from NB to two months of
age and older in this study in response to both abdominal
and facial airstream stimulation follows a developmental
course similar to that which has been documented previously
in the same and other sensory modalities when the infant is
asleep.

Of some relevance is the cardiorespiratory component
of the startle reflex. Landis and Forbes (1934) reported
that the pulse rate was influenced by the phase of the
electrocardiographic cycle in which the startle stimulus
occurred, with more EKG disturbance occurring when the
startle stimulus occurred during atrial systole before the
R-wave. The difficulty of partialing out the effects of
concomitant body movement prevented them from reporting any
consistent change in cardiac rate. More recently, Berg
(1973) elicited the startle reflex acoustically in awake
adults and observed that as the duration of the startle
stimulus increased from 4 to 32 msec the topography of the
HR response became increasingly triphasic. When startle

was elicited by a 50 msec airpuff to the outer canthus of an eye in awake adults a diphasic HR response, which was only measured up to five-seconds post-stimulus onset, was observed (Harbin & Berg, 1983). Therefore, it appears that when the intensity of the startle stimulus was sufficient to elicit the eyeblink component of the startle without the full-blown muscular response the HR response was triphasic.

It has been suggested that the threshold for eliciting a startle reflex is lowered during sleep (Berg, Jackson & Graham, 1975). If this were the case, it could be postulated that the triphasic responses observed in sleeping adults to low and moderately intense stimuli were cardiac components of an elicited startle. Hence it may be that the stimuli which evoked the triphasic response in sleeping infants contained sufficiently rapid transients to elicit startle. Startle may also play a role in explaining the apnea results. The fact that the abdominal airstream resulted in apnea, albeit infrequently, in the infants in this study suggests that perhaps more than one mechanism had a role in inducing apnea in the infants in this study. The startle reflex appears to be one possible mechanism because eyelid contractions and large body movements resembling the Moro or startle reflex were often observed. Skaggs (1926) reported that respiration was often briefly interrupted by the startle stimulus with an ensuing large inspiration followed by irregular breathing patterns with accelerated rate. However, instead of a startle reflex mechanism, Graham and colleagues (in press) have proposed a more general mechanism termed the "transient-detecting interrupt system", which occurs when conditions of stimulus presentation are inappropriate for orienting responses such as during sleep. The critical feature of the eliciting stimulus is its transient aspects and may account for the triphasic HR responses of sleeping infants to low and moderately intense stimuli of varying complexity and duration. Whatever the mechanism, the presence of apneic episodes following instances of LM especially in the NBs suggests that there may be some different mechanism other than the dive reflex which played a role in the production of apnea in the infants in this study. It may be that both the transient-detecting and dive reflex mechanisms mediate the elicited-apnea and that they share a final common effector pathway.

Detection of Infants At-Risk for SIDS

There is considerable evidence that many SIDS victims may be derived from a population of susceptible infants, whereby an infant acutely or chronically exposed to hypoxic conditions may develop faulty cardiorespiratory control. Initially, however, the infant would be expected

to compensate for the hypoxic conditions. Successful
compensatory response may be challenged by complicating
antagonistic conditions such as respiratory infection,
which by itself or in combination with other factors may
induce decompensatory cardiorespiratory response.
Deficiency of regulatory action may result in impaired
function of mechanisms which normally maintain tonic
ventilation. This could be manifested in either
hypoventilation or exagerration of normal reflex responses.

The data yielded in this study indicates that healthy
infants from two to four months of age may be particularly
responsive during sleep to facial airstream stimulation,
exhibiting prolonged elicited-apnea duration and
bradycardia. This is the age of most rapid CNS development
and also corresponds to the age of highest incidence of
SIDS mortality. Moreover, during this time the infants'
sleep states are consolidated and organized, maternal
immunological protection ceases, sensory and perceptual
capabilities dramatically improve and the infant begins to
replace reflexive behavior with purposeful action.
It is reasonable to expect that vulnerability to external
aggravating conditions would be more potentially
deleterious during a time of most rapid development.

The fact that SIDS is more common in the colder winter
months suggests that the role of cold facial stimulation

should receive more attention as a possible contributing factor in the etiology of hypoxia in SIDS victims. We have revealed that cool facial stimulation with an airstream stimulus, which the infant might commonly experience in every day life, can elicit apnea within seconds of stimulus onset. It may be possible to discriminate between healthy infants and infants at-risk for SIDS by eliciting apnea with a facial airstream stimulus. This would be expected to induce a hypoxic and hypercapnic challenge. In the older healthy infants it has been shown that apnea of moderate duration of about 9-12 seconds was elicited. If infants at-risk for SIDS are, as the literature suggests, chronically hypoxic and sluggish to respond to a hypoxic or hypercapnic challenge then one would anticipate deficits in medullary chemoreceptors, carotid body chemoreceptors and/or CNS regions of cardiorespiratory control. It would be predicted, therefore, that during apnea arterial carbon dioxide levels would accumulate and oxygen levels would deplete to a greater extent in these infants than healthy infants before they would respond with resumption of breathing; this would result in observations of more prolonged apnea in the at-risk infants. It has been speculated that SIDS could be a consequence of an exaggerated dive reflex (Wolf, 1966). If this were the case, it might be expected that facial cooling would

elicit apnea on a greater percent of airstream
presentations in the at-risk infants than controls but more
so during the postnatal age of greatest risk, two to four
months. Moreover, the at-risk infants might also display
more pronounced bradycardic responses during apnea,
although, this would be expected solely on the basis of the
anticipated increased duration of apnea.

The advantages of this test are fourfold: 1) it is
simple and does not require extensive training to be able
to administer; 2) it is not time consuming; 3) it is
inexpensive and requires very little equipment; and 4) this
is a test which elicits apnea and as such challenges the
infants central mechanisms of apnea termination and
resumption of breathing. Simply exposing the infants to
various atmospheric concentrations of oxygen and carbon
dioxide only challenges the mechanisms of modulation of
ventilation upon a background of ongoing respiration.
Since the facial airstream interrupts breathing, central
mechanisms, which presumably are the mechanisms of ultimate
failure in the final common pathway in SIDS infants, are
required to reinitiate breathing from respiratory
standstill. Therefore, if an excessive apnea and
concomitant bradycardic response in infants can be uniquely
associated with a pathophysiology in the reflex control of
cardiorespiratory function relating to enhanced

mortality, then diagnostic screening of this type may be of

utility. Specifically, it may be possible to detect a

predisposition to SIDS by analysis of the magnitude of

cardioresiratory change in infants with a history of

prolonged apnea.

Note

1. Graham and coworkers (in press) described this response
as a diphasic deceleration followed by an acceleration.
There are others that have reported a triphasic response
topography (e.g., Berg, Jackson & Graham, 1975). One of
the reasons there is this discrepency is that some studies
have measured only five seconds post-stimulus onset and
consequently missed the late-deceleration which typically
reaches its nadir by about the seventh or eighth post-
stimulus second (e.g., Porges, 1974; Harbin & Berg, 1983).
In addition, another reason for the confusion over the form
of the response may be that the late component is the least
reliable and often appears as a secondary accelerative
phase following a brief return toward pre-trial levels
(e.g., Kearsley, 1973; Ver Hoeve & Leavitt, 1983). In the
studies which examined the topography of the HR response
over at least ten seconds post-stimulus onset the response
predominantly appears as a cubic or quartic trend over
seconds.

APPENDIX A
INFANT BACKGROUND QUESTIONAIRE

The data which we collect from your baby can be affected by a number of factors. The more information we have about your baby, the easier it will be to interpret these data. The following questions are for our use in better understanding your baby's responses, and no individual information will be reported. If you do not wish to answer any question, just leave it blank. Please feel free to ask us to clarify any of the questions.

Today's date _____

Mother's name _____   Mother's Age _____

Infant's name _____   Birth date _____

Birth weight _____

APGAR scores _____

1. Has the baby had any recent colds, ear infections, respiratory difficulties, or any other major health problems? If so, please specify, and provide the approximate dates and durations.

2. Is the baby now taking any medication? If so, what is it, how often and in what dosage is it taken, and what problem is it treating?

3. How many brothers and sisters does the baby have, and what are their ages?

4. If known, was the baby born early, late, or on time? What was the due date?

5. If known, what sort of medication did the mother receive during labor and during birth? If you do not know exactly, please indicate if there were any pills, injections, or gas received.

6. Were there any special problems during pregnancy, such as illnesses, infections, or injuries?

7. Were there any special conditions during birth, such as breech birth, Cesarean section, or use of forceps?

8. Was the Lamaze method used?

9. Where was the baby born?

10. Did the baby have to stay in the hospital for any extra period of time? If so, why?

11. Do you breast-feed your baby?

12. If so, are you taking any medication? If so, what is it, how often and in what dosage is it taken, and what problem is it treating?

APPENDIX B
INFANT STATE RATING SHEET

Stimulus A	A*		F**		F		A		F	
Sequence B	A		A		F		A		F	
Trial No.	1		2		3		4		5	
	pre	post	pre	post	pre	post	pre	post	pre	post
EYES										
open										
closed										
REMs										
MOVEMENT										
none										
small										
large										
VOCALIZATION										
quiet										
soft										
loud										
STATE										
asleep										
?										
drowsy										
?										
alert										
?										
fussy										
?										
crying										

Subject:_____ Date tested:_____ Air temp:_____
Postnatal Age:_____ Rater:_____

* A denotes abdomen
**F denotes face

The following is a list of the remaining stimulus sequence
from trial number 6 to 20 for sequences A and B, respectively.

Sequence A - A,F,F,A,A,F,F,A,A,F,A,F,A,F,A

Sequence B - A,A,F,F,A,F,A,F,A,F,F,A,A,F,F

118

APPENDIX C
INFORMED CONSENT

We are involved in developing a new procedure to test the breathing of young infants. Although our eventual aim is to provide a test that can be used with prematurely born infants, we are interested in results from full-term babies as well. Unfortunately, if breathing problems are present and go undetected, they can have widespread effects on the infant's development and could possibly result in difficulties later on. We would like to explain the procedure we are using to develop the breathing test, and ask your permission for your baby to participate in the research. The information obtained will remain strictly confidential to the extent provided by law. You will have complete access to all information gathered about your infant. As well, if you desire, we will be happy to discuss any conclusions we reach upon completion of this study and send you a summary of the data we collect. The results from this study may be published in a scientific journal concerned with breathing problems of infants.

The basic procedures have been used successfully with infants in the past. What we do is to record heart rate and breathing with small sensors taped to the chest. A short puff of air will be given to the face or stomach area, something like you might do when playing a game by lightly blowing in the baby's face. None of the sensors nor the air puff produce any discomfort or danger. In fact, in most circumstances we will want to carry out the test while the baby is asleep. The entire test lasts about one hour.

Because the test is still being developed, we probably will not have specific information about your baby's breathing, but should we find a suggestion of a difficulty we will inform you. There are no risks or discomforts expected. You will receive five dollars for participating in this project.

If you have any further questions now or at any other point, we will be happy to answer them. If at any time you decide to withdraw consent or discontinue participation you are, of course, free to do so.

I understand that if my infant is injured during this study, and if the investigator is at fault, the University of Florida and the Board of Regents of the State of Florida shall be liable only as provided by law. I understand that I may seek appropriate compensation for injury by contacting the Insurance Coordinator at 107 Tigert Hall, University of Florida, telephone number 392-1325.

I have read and understand the above described procedure
in which my intent is to participate and have received a copy
of this description. I agree to alllow my infant
child, _____(baby's name), to participate in the above
described research.

subject_____ date____ witness_____ date____

_____ Investigator_____ date____

(relationship to subject)

APPENDIX D
ANALYSIS OF THE PERCENT OF TRIALS WITH QS, TS AND AS STATES

The following analyses were all ANOVAs, which examined the percent of face and abdomen trials in which infants were in QS, TS and AS, with Age (i.e., NB vs. 2-4 vs. 8-12) as the between-subject factor and Site of stimuluation (i.e., face vs. abdomen) and State (i.e., QS vs. AS vs. TS) as within-subject factors. The results of this analysis only revealed a significant interaction between State and Age, $F(4/98)=7.9$, $p<.001$. Subanalysis consisted of dividing the analyses into QS and non-QS data. The analysis of QS yielded a significant Age effect, $F(2/49)=8.1$, $p<.001$, which was due to less QS displayed by the NBs than by 2-4 infants, $F(1/35)=8.4$, $p<.01$, and no difference between the 2-4 and 8-12 groups. The analysis of the non-QS data (i.e., percent of trials in AS and TS) revealed a significant interaction between State and Age, $F(2/49)=6.8$, $p<.005$. Follow-up analyses revealed greater percentage of AS in the NBs than in the 2-4 infants, $F(1/35)=8.4$, $p<.01$; however, no significant difference in the percentage of either AS or TS emerged when the two older groups were compared. Therefore, in sum, infants spent a predominant amount of time in QS throughout the testing session. The

NBs displayed a slightly greater tendency to be in AS than the 2-4 or 8-12 infants. In any case, the infants showed no tendency to be in any particular state when a face or abdominal airpuff was delivered.

To determine if there was any sleep state pattern during the session, an analysis of State was performed comparing the state ratings (i.e., 2 for AS, 1 for TS and 0 for QS) across Trials, ignoring stimulus Site. Figure 1 depicts these mean state ratings across the 20-trial session. The initial analysis constrasted State across the first 10 trials for all age groups. Since each infant had at least 10 trials, all 52 infants could be included in the analysis. A significant Age-by-Trial interaction, $F(18/441)=2.2$, $p<.005$, emerged. An independent orthogonal trend analysis of each age group revealed significant decreasing linear trends across Trials for NBs, $F(1/13)=7.5$, $p<.05$, and for 2-4s, $F(1/22)=8.2$, $p<.01$; but the analysis of the 8-12 infants did not demonstrate a significant change across Trials, $F(9/126)=1.6$, indicating a greater tendency for the younger infants to be in AS or TS at the beginning of testing.

The next analysis investigated whether the state of the infants changed during the last 10 trials. It included only those subjects in each age group who completed at least 18 trials. This analysis revealed only a significant increasing linear trend across Trials, $F(1/36)=4.2$, $p<.05$, indicating that the infants demonstrated a gradual change of state toward AS from QS at the end of the session. Figure 1 displays these trends also.

APPENDIX E
ANALYSIS OF THE PERCENT OF TRIALS WITH LARGE MOVEMENT

Table 5 presents the mean percent of trials in which LM was observed across age group in response to the airstream stimulus to the face and the abdomen. The analyses of the percent of face and abdomen trials in which LM was observed were all ANOVAs with Age as the between-subject factor and Site of stimulation, State (QS vs. all states collapsed) and presence or absence of LM as the three within-subject factors. Neither the effect of State, nor any of the interactions of State with Age, Conditions or LM were significant, indicating that the frequency of LM was not affected by the inclusion of non-QS data in the sample. There was, however, a significant interaction between Age, Site and LM, $F(2/49)=3.7$, $p<.05$.

Follow-up analyses consisted of comparing whether stimulus site differentially influenced the percent of elicited-LM in the 2-4 and 8-12 infants; it did not, $F(1/36)=0.5$. However, while there was greater percent of LM produced by the 2-4 infants than by the 8-12 infants, $F(1/36)=350.4$, $p<.001$, there was a much greater percent of trials with no LM than trials with LM, $F(1/35)=91.1$, $p<.001$. This was not the case for the NB infants who displayed greater percent of trials with LM than the two older groups, $F(1/35)=54.6$, $p<.001$; the NBs also produced a greater proportion of trials with LM relative to the percent of trials with no LM observed. This was confirmed in an analysis of only the NB group by a significant Site-by-LM interaction, $F(1/13)=7.1$, $p<.05$. This interaction was due to a significantly less percent of abdomen trials with LM than abdomen trials with no LM, $F(1/13)=7.4$, $p<.05$; whereas no differences were found between the percent of face trials with LM and face trials with no LM.

In sum, there was more LM elicited in the NBs than the 2-4 infants, who in turn displayed more elicited LM than the 8-12 infants. Overall there were many more trials with no LM elicited than trials with LM. It was only the NB group which displayed more sensitivity to the facial airpuff, with more elicited LM than to the abdominal airpuff.

APPENDIX F
ANALYSIS OF THE HR RESPONSE TO THE AIRSTREAM STIMULUS:
FACE VS. ABDOMEN

To examine whether there were any differences between age groups and stimulus sites in the HR response during the ten seconds of airstream presentation the following analyses were performed. Within the first second post-stimulus onset there was a brief early-deceleration. An ANACOVA on second one revealed only an Age effect, $F(2/46)=6.4$, $p<.005$. Subanalyses indicated that the two older groups of infants displayed a greater initial deceleration than the NBs. This was revealed when the two younger groups were separately analysed; there was a significant Age effect, $F(1/32)=5.7$, $p<.05$, found, but no significant difference was found when the two older groups were compared. Additionally, the NBs' HR for second one did not significantly change from pretrial levels, $t(12)=0.21$. Therefore, both the 2-4 and the 8-12 groups decelerated within the first second after airstream onset to mean HR levels of -1.21 and -2.75 bpm, respectively, regardless of whether the airstream was directed to the face or abdomen. The NBs, on the otherhand, displayed no change in HR level during this time.

The acceleration component was evaluated by analysing the third second post-stimulus onset. Only a significant stimulation Site effect, $F(1/46)=4.7$, $p<.05$, was found, indicating that age did not significantly influence magnitude but that there was greater HR acceleration to the facial airpuff than the abdominal airpuff, with mean adjusted HR bpm values of 4.25 and 3.04 respectively. However, this conclusion was not quite accurate because the older infants accelerated from below pretrial level while the NBs did not. Therefore, the infants displayed differing rates of acceleration across seconds 1, 2 and 3. Accordingly, analyses revealed that the 8-12 group exhibited a faster rate of acceleration than the 2-4 group, which accelerated faster than the NBs, as indicated by respective significant two-way interactions of Age and Seconds of $F(2/70)=7.3$ and $F(2/66)=6.1$, both at $p<.005$.

The subsequent late-deceleration was analysed using seconds 3 to 10. The initial ANACOVA yielded interactions between Age and Site, $F(2/46)=3.1$, $p<.05$, and Seconds and Site, $F(7/329)=2.5$, both significant at $p<.05$. When the NB and 8-12 groups were contrasted only a significant interaction between Age and Seconds, $F(7/182)=6.3$, $p<.001$, remained, indicating that HR decelerated to a greater magnitude in the 8-12 infants than the NBs. In fact, separate t-tests over seconds 3 to 10 for the NB infants revealed that HR only returned to pretrial levels from the previous acceleration and did not significantly decelerate. Moreover, since none of the effects which included Site reached significance, it can be concluded that neither of these groups responded differentially to either airpuff during this interval. However, when the 2-4 group was separately analysed the significant interaction between Sites and a quadratic trend over Seconds, $F(1/21)=6.4$, $p<.05$, remained, indicating that the former interactions with the Sites factor were due to greater deceleration elicited by the facial airpuff than by the abdominal airpuff in these infants.

The analysis of the HR trends during the seconds 11 to 25 of stimulus offset only revealed significant main effects of Age, $F(2/46)=7.1$, $p<.005$, Seconds, $F(14/658)=5.7$, $p<.001$, and their two-way interaction, $F(28/658)=2.4$, $p<.001$. An orthogonal trend analysis revealed that this interaction arose from cubic trends over Seconds, $F(2/47)=3.7$, $p<.05$, indicating that in response to the offset of either facial or abdominal airpuff each age group displayed a similar cubic trend in HR (i.e., a recovery toward pretrial levels, then a brief decrement in HR followed by continued recovery toward pretrial levels).

REFERENCES

Adkinson, C.D., & Berg, W.K. Cardiac deceleration in
    newborns: Habituation, dishabituation, and offset
    responses. Journal of Experimental Child Psychology, 1976,
    21, 46-60.

Allen, L.G., Howard, G., Smith, J.B., McCubbin, J.A., &
    Weaver, R.L. Infant heart rate response to trigeminal
    airstream stimulation: Determination of normal and deviant
    values. Pediatric Research, 1979, 13, 184-187.

Anderson, H.T. The reflex nature of the physiological
    adjustments to diving and their afferent pathway. Acta
    Physiologica Scandinavica, 1963, 58, 263-273.

Ariagno, R.L., Guilleminault, C., Baldwin, R., & Owen-
    Boeddiker, M. Movement and gastroesophageal reflux in awake
    term infants with near miss SIDS, unrelated to apnea.
    Journal of Pediatrics, 1982, 100, 894-897.

Benjamin, L.S. Facts and artifacts in using analysis of
    covariance to "undo" the law of initial values.
    Psychophysiology, 1967, 4, 187-202.

Bergman, A.B., Beckwith, J.B., & Ray, C.G. Part II.
    Epidemiology. Proceedings of the second international
    conference on causes of sudden death in infants. Seattle:
    University of Washington Press, 1970, Pp. 25-79.

Berg, K.M. Elicitation of acoustic startle in the human.
    Universtiy of Wisconsin, 1973. Dissertation Abstracts
    International, 1974, 34B(10), 5217.

Berg, K.M., Berg, W.K., & Graham, F.K. Infant heart rate
    response as a function of stimulus and state.
    Psychophysiology, 1971, 8, 30-44.

Berg, W.K., & Berg, K.M. Psychophysiological development in infancy: State, sensory function and attention. In J. Osofsky (Ed.) Handbook of Infant Development. New York: Wiley, 1979, Pp. 283-343.

Berg, W.K., Jackson, J.C., & Graham, F.K. Tone intensity and rise-decay time effects on cardiac responses during sleep. Psychophysiology, 1975, 12, 254-261.

Boychuk, R.B., Rigatto, H., & Seshia, M.M.K. The effect of lung inflation on the control of respiratory frequency of the neonate. Journal of Physiology (London), 1977, 270, 653-660.

Brady, J.P., Ariagno, J.L., Watts, J.C., Goldman, S.L., & Dumpit, T.M. Apnea, hypoxemia and aborted sudden infant death syndrome. Pediatrics, 1978, 62, 686-691.

Brand, M.M., & Bignami, A. The effects of chronic hypoxia on the neonatal and infantile brain: A neuropathological study of five premature infants with the respiratory distress syndrome treated by prolonged artificial ventilation. Brain, 1969, 92, 233-254.

Brooks, J.G. Apnea of infancy and sudden infant death syndrome. American Journal of Diseases in Children, 1982, 136, 1012-1023.

Brooks, J.G., Schluete, M.A., Nabelet, Y., & Tooley, W.H. Sleep state and arterial blood gases and pH in human newborn and young infants. Journal of Perinatal Medicine, 1978, 6, 280-286.

Brown, W.V., Ostheimer, G.W., Bell, G.C., & Datta, S.S. Newborn response to oxygen blown over the face. Anesthesiology, 1976, 44, 535-536.

Coons, M.A., & Guilleminault, M.D. Development of sleep-wake patterns and non-rapid eye movement sleep stages during the first six months of life in normal infants. Pediatrics, 1982, 69, 793-798.

Cordero, L., Jr., & Hon, E.H. Neonatal bradycardia following nasopharyngeal stimulation. Journal of Pediatrics, 1971, 78, 441-447.

Dejours, P. Control of respiration by arterial chemoreceptors. Annals of the New York Academy of Science, 1963, 109, 682-695.

Downing, S.E., & Lee, J.C. Laryngeal chemosensitivity: A possible mechanism for sudden infant death syndrome. Journal of Pediatrics, 1981, 98, 791-794.

Elsner, R., Franklin, D.L., Van Citters, R.L., & Kenney, D.W. Cardiovascular defense against asphyxia. Science, 1966, 153, 141-149.

Furedy, J.J., Morrison, J.W., Heslegrave, R.J., & Arabian, J.M. Effects of water temperature on some noninvasively measured components of the human dive reflex: An experimental response-topography analysis. Psychophysiology, 1983, 20, 569-578.

Getts, A.G., & Hill, F.H. Sudden infant death syndrome: Incidence at various altitudes. Developmental Medicine and Child Neurology, 1982, 24, 61-68.

Graham, F.K. Constraints on measuring heart rate and period sequentially through real and cardiac time. Psychophysiology, 1978, 15, 492-495.

Graham, F.K., Anthony, B.J., & Zeigler, B.L. The orienting response and developmental processes. In D. Siddle (Ed.), The Orienting Response. Sussex, England: Wiley, in press.

Greenhouse, S.W., & Geisser, S. On methods in the analysis of profile data. Psychometrica, 1959, 24, 95-112.

Gregory, G.A. Resuscitation of the newborn. Anesthesiology, 1975, 43, 225-237.

Guilleminault, C., Ariagno, R., Korobkin, R., Coons, S., Owen-Boeddiker, M., & Baldwin, R. Sleep parameters and respiratory variables in "near miss" sudden infant death syndrome infants. Pediatrics, 1981, 68, 354-360.

Guilleminault,C., Ariagno,R., Korobkin, R., Nagel, L., Baldwin, R., Coons, S., & Owen, M. Mixed and obstructive sleep apnea and near miss for sudden infant death syndrome: 2. Comparison of near miss and normal control infants by age. Pediatrics, 1979, 64, 882-891.

Guilleminault, C., Souquet, M., Ariagno, D.L., Korobkin, R., & Simmons, F.B. Five cases of near-miss sudden infant death syndrome and development of obstructive sleep apnea syndrome. Pediatrics, 1984, 73, 71-78.

Guyton, A.C. Textbook of Medical Physiology. Philadelphia: Saunders Co., 1981, Pp. 623.

Haddad, G.G., Epstein, M.A.F., Epstein, R.A., Mazza, N.M., Mellins, R.B., & Krongrad, E. The QT interval in aborted sudden infant death syndrome infants. Pediatric Research, 1979, 13, 136-138.

Haddad, G.G., Leistner, H.L., Lai, T.L., & Mellins, R.B. Ventilation and ventilatory pattern during sleep in aborted sudden infant death syndrome. Pediatric Research, 1981, 15, 879-883.

Haddad, G.G., Schaeffer, J.I., & Bazzy, A.R. Postnatal maturation of the ventilatory response to hypoxia. In J.R. Sutton, C.S. Houston & N.L. Jones (Eds.), Hypoxia, exercise, and altitude: Proceedings of the third Banff international hypoxia symposium. New York: Liss Inc., 1983, Pp. 39-50.

Haddad, G.G., Walsh, E.M., Leistner, H.L., Grodin, W.K., & Mellins, R.B. Abnormal maturation of sleep states in infants with aborted sudden infant death syndrome. Pediatric Research, 1981, 15, 1055-1057.

Haidmayer, R., Kurz, R., Kenner, T., Wurm, H., & Pfeiffer, K.P. Physiological and clinical aspects of respiration control in infants with relation to the sudden infant death syndrome. Klinische Wochenschrift, 1982, 60, 9-18.

Harbin, T.J., & Berg, W.K. The effects of age and prestimulus duration upon reflex inhibition. Psychophysiology, 1983, 20, 603-610.

Harper, R.M. Neurophysiology of sleep. In J.R. Sutton, C.S. Houston & N.L. Jones (Eds.), Hypoxia, exercise, and altitude: Proceedings of the third Banff international hypoxia symposium. New York: Liss Inc., 1983, Pp. 65-73.

Harper, R.M., Frostig, Z., Taube, D., Hoppenbrouwers, T., & Hodgman, J.E. Development of sleep-waking temporal sequencing in infants at risk for the sudden infant death syndrome. Experimental Neurology, 1983, 79, 821-829.

Harper, R.M., Leake, B., Hodgman, J.E., & Hoppenbrouwers, T. Developmental patterns of heart rate and heart rate variability during sleep and waking in normal infants and infants at risk for the sudden infant death syndrome. Sleep, 1982, 5, 28-38.

Harper, R.M., Leake, B., Hoppenbrouwers, T., Sterman, M.B., McGinty, D.J., & Hodgman, J. Polygraphic studies of normal infants and infants at risk for the sudden infant death syndrome. Pediatric Research, 1978, 12, 778-785.

Harper, R.M., & Sieck, G.C. Discharge correlations between neurons in the nucleus parabrachialis medialis during sleep and waking states. Brain Research, 1980, 199, 343-358.

Henderson-Smart, D.J. Regulation of breathing in the perinatal period. In N.A. Saunders & C.E. Sullivan (Eds.), Sleep and breathing, New York: Marcel Dekker Inc., 1984, Pp. 423-455.

Henderson-Smart, D.J., & Read, D.J.C. Depression of intercostal and abdominal muscle activity and vulnerability to asphyxia during active sleep in the newborn. In C. Guilleminault and W.C. Dement (Eds.), Sleep Apnea Syndromes, New York: Liss Inc., 1978, 93-117.

Herbst, J.J., Minton, S., & Book, L.S. Gastroesophageal reflux causing respiratory distress and apnea in newborn infants. Journal of Pediatrics, 1979, 95, 763.

Hodgman, J.E., Hoppenbrouwers, T., Geidel, S., Hadeed, A., Sterman, M.B., Harper, R., & McGinty, D. Respiratory behavior in near-miss sudden infant death syndrome. Pediatrics, 1982, 69, 785-792.

Hoppenbrouwers, T., & Hodgman, J.E. Sudden infant death syndrome (SIDS): An integration of ontogenetic pathologic, physiologic and epidemiologic factors. Neuropediatrics, 1982, 13, 36-51.

Hoppenbrouwers, T., Hodgman, J.E., Arakawa, K., Harper, R., & Sterman, M.B. Respiration during the first six months of life in normal infants. III. Computer identification of breathing pauses. Pediatric Research, 1980, 14, 1230-1233.

Hoppenbrouwers, T., Hodgman, J.E., Harper, R.M., & Sterman, M.B. Fetal heart rates in siblings of infants with sudden infant death syndrome. Obstetrics and Gynecology, 1981, 58, 319-325.

Hoppenbrouwers, T., Hodgman, J.E., McGinty, D., Harper, R.M., & Sterman, M.B. Sudden infant death syndrome: Sleep apnea and respiration in subsequent siblings. Pediatrics, 1980, 66, 205-214.

Hoppenbrouwers, T., Jenson, D.K., Hodgman, J.E., Harper, R.M., & Sterman, M.B. The emergence of a circadian pattern in respiratory rates: Comparison between control infants and subsequent siblings of SIDS. Pediatric Research, 1980, 14, 345-351.

Hoppenbrouwers, T., Zanini, B., & Hodgman, J.E. Intrapartum fetal heart rate and sudden infant death syndrome. American Journal of Obstetrics and Gynecology, 1979, 133, 217-220.

Hunt, C.E. Abnormal hypercarbic and hypoxic sleep arousal responses in near-miss SIDS infants. Pediatric Research, 1981, 15, 1462-1464.

Hunt, C.E., McCulloch, K., & Brouillette, R.T. Diminished hypoxic ventilatory responses in near-miss sudden infant death syndrome. Journal of Applied Physiology: Respiration, Environmental and Exercise Physiology, 1981, 50, 1313-1317.

Hurwitz, B., & Furedy, J.J. The human dive reflex: An experimental topographical and physiological analysis. Psychophysiology, 1979, 16, 192. (Abstract)

Irving, L., Solandt, D.Y., Solandt, O.M., & Fisher, K.C. The respiratory metabolism of the seal and its adjustments to diving. Journal of Cellular and Comparative Physiology, 1935, 7, 137-151.

Katona, P.G., Frasz, A., & Egbert, J. Maturation of cardiac control in full-term and preterm infants during sleep. Early Human Development, 1980, 4, 145-159.

Kaun, A., Blum, D., Engelman, E., & Waterschoot, P. Effects of central apneas on transcutaneous PO2 in control subjects, siblings of victims of sudden infant death syndrome, and near-miss infants. Pediatrics, 1982, 69, 413-418.

Kawakami, Y., Natelson, B.H., & DuBois, A.B. Cardiovascular effects of face immersion and factors affecting diving reflex in man. Journal of Applied Physiology, 1967, 23, 964-970.

Kelly, D.H., & Shannon, D.C. Periodic breathing in infants with near-miss sudden infant death syndrome. Pediatrics, 1979, 63, 355-360.

Kelly, D.H., & Shannon, D.C. Sudden infant death syndrome and near sudden infant death syndrome: A review of the literature, 1964 to 1982. Pediatric Clinics of North America, 1982, 29, 1241-1261.

Kelly, D.H., Twanmoh, J., & Shannon, D.C. Incidence of apnea in siblings of sudden infant death syndrome victims studied at home. Pediatrics, 1982, 70, 128-131.

Kelly, D.H., Walker, A.M., Cahen, L., & Shannon, D.C. Periodic breathing in siblings of sudden infant death syndrome victims. Pediatrics, 1980, 66, 515-520.

Kirkpatrick, S.M.L., Olinsky, A., Bryan, M.H., & Bryan, A.C. Effect of premature delivery on the maturation of the Hering-Breuer inspiratory inhibitory reflex in human infants. Journal of Pediatrics, 1976, 88, 1010-1014.

Kuich, T.E., & Zimmerman, D. Endorphins, ventilatory control and sudden infant death syndrome--A review and synthesis. Medical Hypotheses, 1981, 7, 1231-1240.

Landis, C., & Forbes, T.W. The relation of startle reactions to the cardiac cycle. Psychiatric Quarterly, 1934, 8, 235-242.

Leistner, H.L., Haddad, G.G., Epstein, R.A., Lai, T.L., Epstein, M.A.F., Eng, S.D., & Mellins, R.B. Heart rate and heart rate variability during sleep in aborted sudden infant death syndrome. Journal of Pediatrics, 1980, 97, 51-55.

Lipton, E.L., Steinschneider, A., & Richmond, J.B. Autonomic function in the neonate: VII. Maturational changes in cardiac control. Child Development, 1966, 37, 1-16.

Maloney, J.E., & Bowes, G. The effect of hypoxia on the fetal respiratory system. In J.R. Sutton, C.S. Houston & N.L. Jones (Eds.), Hypoxia, exercise, and altitude: Proceedings of the third Banff international hypoxia symposium. New York: Liss Inc., 1983, Pp. 17-37.

Marotta, F., Fort, M., Mondestin, H., Hiatt, I.M., & Hegyi, T. The response to CO2 in infants at risk for SIDS. Pediatric Research, 1984, 16, 327A. (Abstract)

McCubbin, J.A., Smith, J.B., Allen, L.G., Wood, F.B., & McGraw, C.P. Bradycardia in the early neonatal period: The diving reflex and trigeminal airstream stimulation. Psychophysiology, 1977, 14, 111. (Abstract)

McGinty, D.J., & Beahm, E.K. Neurobiology of sleep. In N.A. Saunders & C.E. Sullivan (Eds.), Sleep and breathing. New York: Marcel Dekker Inc., 1984, Pp. 1-89.

McGinty, D.J., & Sterman, M.B. Sleep physiology, hypoxemia, and the sudden infant death syndrome. Sleep, 1980, 3, 361-373..

Mellins, R.B., & Haddad, G.G. Cardiorespiratory control in sudden infant death syndrome. In J.R. Sutton, C.S. Houston & N.L. Jones (Eds.), Hypoxia, exercise, and altitude: Proceedings of the third Banff international hypoxia symposium. New York: Liss Inc., 1983, Pp. 51-56.

Moore, A. The sudden infant death syndrome. British Journal of Hospital Medicine, 1981, 26, 37-45.

Myers, R.E. Two patterns of perinatal brain damage and their conditions of occurrence. American Journal of Obstetrics and Gynecology. 1972, 112, 246-276.

Naeye, R.L. Pulmonary arterial abnormalities in the sudden infant death syndrome. New England Journal of Medicine. 1973, 289, 1167-1170.

Naeye, R.L. Brain-stem and adrenal abnormalities in the sudden-infant-death syndrome. American Journal of Clinical Pathology, 1976, 66, 526-530.

Naeye, R.L., Fisher, R., Ryser, M., & Whalen, P. Carotid body in sudden infant death syndrome. Science, 1976, 91, 567-569.

Naeye, R.L., Whalen, P., Ryser, M., & Fisher, R. Cardiac and other abnormalities in the sudden infant death syndrome. American Journal of Pathology, 1976, 82, 1-8.

Parmelee, A.H., Stern, E., & Harris, M.A. Maturation of respiration in prematures and young infants. Neuropadiatrie, 1972, 3, 294-303.

Peterson, D.R. Evolution of the epidemiology of sudden infant death syndrome. Epidemiologic Reviews, 1980, 2, 97-112.

Pomerleau-Malcuit, A., & Clifton, R.K. Neonatal heart-rate response to tactile, auditory, and vestibular stimulation in different states. Child Development, 1973, 44, 485-496.

Porges, S.W. The application of spectral analysis for the detection of fetal distress. In T.M. Fields, A.M. Sostek, S. Goldberg, & H.H. Shuman (Eds.), Infants born at risk. New York: Spectrum, 1979.

Porges, S.W., Stamps, L.E., & Walter, G.F. Heart rate variability and newborn heart rate responses to illumination changes. Developmental Psychology, 1974, 10, 507-513.

Prechtl, H.F.R. The behavioral states of the newborn infant (a review). Brain Research, 1974, 76, 185-212.

Prystowsky, E.N., Jackman, W.M., Rickenberger, R.L., Heger, J.J., & Zipes, D.P. Effect of autonomic blockade on ventricular refractoriness and atrioventricular nodal conduction in humans: Evidence supporting a direct cholinergic action on ventricular muscle refractoriness. Circulation Research, 1981, 49, 511-518.

Rabinovitch, M., Gamble, W., Nadas, A.S., Meittinen, Q.S., & Reid, L. Rat pulmonary circulation after chronic hypoxia: Hemodynamic and structural features. American Journal of Physiology, 1979, 236, 818-827.

Rappaport, L., Kozakewich, H.P.W., Fenton, T., Mandell, F., Vawter, G.F., & Yang, H.Y. Cerebrospinal fluid met-enkephalin in sudden infant death syndrome. Pediatric Research, 1984, 16, 231A. (Abstract)

Rewey, H.H. Developmental change in infant heart rate response during sleeping and waking states. Developmental Psychology, 1973, 8, 35-41.

Richards, J.E. The statistical analysis of heart rate: A review emphasizing infancy data. Psychophysiology, 1980, 17, 153-166.

Richardson, P.S., & Peatfield, A.C. Reflexes concerned in the defence of the lungs. Bulletin of European Physiopathology and Respiration, 1981, 17, 979-1012.

Rigatto, H. Ventilatory response to hypoxia. Seminar in Perinatology, 1977, 1, 357-362.

Rigatto, H. Apnea. Pediatric Clinics of North America, 1982, 29, 1105-1116.

Sachis, P.N., Armstrong, D.L., Becker, L.E., & Bryan, A.C. The vagus nerve and sudden infant death syndrome: A morphometric study. Journal of Pediatrics, 1981, 98, 278-280.

Sameroff, A.J., Cashmore, T.F., & Dykes, A.C. Heart rate deceleration during visual fixation in human newborns. Developmental Psychology, 1973, 8 117-119.

Schulte, F.J., Albani, M., Schmizer, H., & Bentele, K. Neuronal control of neonatal respiration-sleep apnea and the sudden infant death syndrome. Neuropediatrics, 1982, 13, 3-14.

Shannon, D.C. Pathophysiologic mechanisms causing sleep apnea and hypoventilation in infants. Sleep, 1980, 3, 343-348.

Shannon, D.C., & Kelly, D.H. SIDS and near-SIDS (second of two parts). New England Journal of Medicine, 1982, 306, 1022-1028.

Shannon, D.C., & Kelly, D.H. Sudden Infant Death Syndrome. In N.A. Saunders & C.E. Sullivan (Eds.), Sleep and breathing, New York: Marcel Dekker Inc., 1984, Pp. 457-484.

Shannon, D.C., Kelly, D.H., & O'Connell, K. Abnormal regulation of ventilation in infants at risk for sudden infant death syndrome. New England Journal of Medicine, 1977, 297, 747-750.

Skaggs, E.B. Changes in pulse, breathing and steadiness under conditions of startledness and excited expectancy. Journal of Comparative Psychology, 1926, 6, 303-318.

Stevens, J.C., Marks, L.E., & Simonson, D.C. Regional sensitivity and spatial summation in the warmth sense. Physiology and Behavior, 1974, 13, 825-836.

Song, S.H., Lee, W.K., Chung, Y.A., & Hong, S.K. Mechanism of apneic bradycardia in man. Journal of Applied Physiology, 1969, 27, 323-327.

Steinschneider, A. Prolonged apnea and the sudden infant death syndrome: Clinical and laboratory observations. Pediatrics, 1972, 50, 646-654.

Steinschneider, A. Prolonged apnea and respiratory instability: A discriminative study. Pediatrics, 1977, 59, 962-970.

Sterman, M.B., Harper, R.M., Hoppenbrouwers, T., McGinty, D.J., & Hodgman, J.E. Quantitative comparison of EEG development during sleep in infants at high and low risk for the sudden infant death syndrome. Sleep Research, 1979, 9, 132. (Abstract)

Takashima, S., Armstrong, D., Becker, L.E., & Bryan, A.C. Cerebral hypoperfusion in the sudden infant death syndrome? Brainstem gliosis and vasculature. Annals of Neurology, 1978, 4, 257-262.

Taylor, W.B. A single risk factor in sudden infant death and its multiple attack distribution. International Journal of Epidemiology, 1982, 11, 138-145.

Valdes-Dapena, M.A. Sudden infant death syndrome: A review of the medical literature 1974-1979. Pediatrics, 1980, 66, 597-614.

Valdes-Dapena, M.A., Gillane, M.M., Cassady, J.C., Catherman, R., & Ross, D. Wall thickness of small pulmonary arteries: Its measurement in victims of sudden infant death syndrome. Archives of Pathological and Laboratory Medicine, 1980, 104, 621-624.

Ver Hoeve, J.N., & Leavitt, L.A. Neonatal acoustically-elicited cardiac response: Modulation by state and antecedent stimulation. Manuscript submitted for publication, 1983.

Walsh, J.K., Farrell, M.L., Keenan, W.G., Lucas, M., & Kramer, M. Gastroesophageal reflux in infants: Relation to apnea. Journal of Pediatrics, 1981, 99, 197.

Wilder, J. The law of initial values. Psychosomatic Medicine, 1950, 12, 392.

Wilds, P.L. Observations of intrauterine fetal breathing movements--A review. American Journal of Obstetrics and Gynecology, 1978, 131, 315-338.

Williams, A., Vawter, G., & Reid, L. Increased muscularity of the pulmonary circulation in victims of the sudden infant death syndrome. Pediatrics, 1979, 63, 18-23.

Wolf, S. Sudden death and the oxygen-conserving reflex. American Heart Journal, 1966, 71, 840-841.

BIOGRAPHICAL SKETCH

Barry Elliot Hurwitz, the fourth son of William and Ruth Hurwitz, was conceived in love but with questionable planning and born on March 18, 1956 in Windsor, Ontario, Canada, seven years after the birth of number three son, Michael. Due to the age difference between him and his brothers (i.e., Paul, Richard and Michael), most of Barry's formative years were spent as an only child. However, one shouldn't despair because this meant that Barry was the sole beneficiary of parents skilled in the art of manipulating reinforcement contingencies. The diligent use of these skills resulted in the enhancement of Barry's self-confidence and self-esteem, which promoted his successful completion of five years of high school (i.e., grades 9 to 13) in four. Barry graduated from Vincent Massey High School in June of 1974 and received an Ontario Scholarship for academic achievement.

Leaving the air-polluted auto-town of Windsor for the glamor of big city life, Barry enrolled at the University of Toronto to study what makes people tick. Being influenced by the strongly behavioristic psychology department, Barry was biased against the use of hypothetical constructs and drawn to physiological processes in the study of the interdependency of the brain and the body. One day, while present at a noon-hour brown-bag seminar, Barry experienced his first taste of the excitement of the proverbial pursuit of knowledge, which was to influence his research interests from then until the present. At this seminar a film was presented by Dr. David Jones visiting from the University of British Columbia. Half the screen depicted the forcible immersion of the head of a duck into a bucket of water, while the other half displayed the polygraph recordings of the physiological responses. Upon immersion Barry observed that the duck's heart rate decelerated to about 10% of its resting level. This was quite an amazing response, which he later discovered was termed the diving reflex. Being in the process of conditioning large-magnitude decelerations in human adults and meeting with some difficulty, Barry wondered if he could somehow utilize this reflex in humans, since it represented a remarkable integration of cardiorespiratory mechanisms. Ever since this day and after his graduation from the University of Toronto, with an Honors B. Sc. degree in psychology and zoology, Barry has pursued the human dive reflex as it exists in human adults and infants.

Barry received his M.S. degree from Ohio University in 1978 in psychophysiology and then transferred to the

University of Florida to study physiological psychology and infants. He was awarded a post-graduate scholarship from the Natural Science and Engineering Research Council of Canada in 1981, which along with a fellowship from the Graduate School supported his final years of graduate work. In April of 1983 Barry's study of infants expanded into a personal interest, with the birth of his and his wife Debbie's first son, Joseph Henry. Joseph attempted to participate in this study but with true wisdom (probably inherited from his father) decided that he preferred to sleep in his own bed rather than in the sterile confines of the laboratory. Under the astute aegis of Dr. W. Keith Berg, Barry received his Ph.D. in August of 1984 with an emphasis on cardiovascular and developmental physiological psychology. Barry will continue his study of the central neural basis for cardiorespiratory physiology as a postdoctoral research associate with Dr. Neil Schneiderman at the University of Miami in Coral Gables, Florida.

I certify that I have read this study and that in my opinion it conforms to acceptable standards of scholarly presentation and is fully adequate, in scope and quality, as a dissertation for the degree of Doctor of Philosophy.

W. Keith Berg, Chairman
Associate Professor of Psychology

I certify that I have read this study and that in my opinion it conforms to acceptable standards of scholarly presentation and is fully adequate, in scope and quality, as a dissertation for the degree of Doctor of Philosophy.

Merle E. Meyer
Professor of Psychology

I certify that I have read this study and that in my opinion it conforms to acceptable standards of scholarly presentation and is fully adequate, in scope and quality, as a dissertation for the degree of Doctor of Philosophy.

Peter Lang
Associate Professor of Clinical
Psychology

I certify that I have read this study and that in my opinion it conforms to acceptable standards of scholarly presentation and is fully adequate, in scope and quality, as a dissertation for the degree of Doctor of Philosophy.

Philip Posner
Associate Professor of Physiology

I certify that I have read this study and that in my opinion it conforms to acceptable standards of scholarly presentation an is fully adequate, in scope and quality, as a dissertation for the degree of Doctor of Philosophy.

Neil Rowland
Associate Professor of Psychology

This dissertation was submitted to the Graduate Faculty of the Department of Psychology in the College of Liberal Arts and Sciences and to the Graduate School, and was accepted as partial fulfillment of the requirements for the degree of Doctor of Philosophy.

August, 1984

_____
Dean, Graduate School

CPSIA information can be obtained
at www.ICGtesting.com
Printed in the USA
BVHW052123090619
550551BV00008B/264/P